THE BIG BOOK OF BIBLE GAMES AND PUZZLES

By JOY MacKENZIE & SHIRLEY BLEDSOE

with SHANA, KRISTEN, MELISSA & AMANDA

Illustrated by DONICÉ

Zondervan Books
Zondervan Publishing House
Grand Rapids, Michigan

All student activity pages are designed to be used by individual students. Permission is hereby granted to the purchaser of one copy of **THE BIG BOOK OF BIBLE GAMES AND PUZZLES** to reproduce copies of these pages in sufficient quantity for use by the students in one classroom.

PERMISSION GRANTED

Cover design and additional art by Maribeth Wright.

THE BIG BOOK OF BIBLE GAMES AND PUZZLES
© Copyright 1982 by The Zondervan Corporation, Grand Rapids, Michigan.

Zondervan Books are published by Zondervan
Publishing House, 1415 Lake Drive, S.E.,
Grand Rapids, Michigan 49506

ISBN 0-310-70271-2

Printed in the United States of America

87 88 89 90 91 92 / 15 14 13 12 11 10 9 8 7

This SUPerTeRRIFic book

belongs to: _____

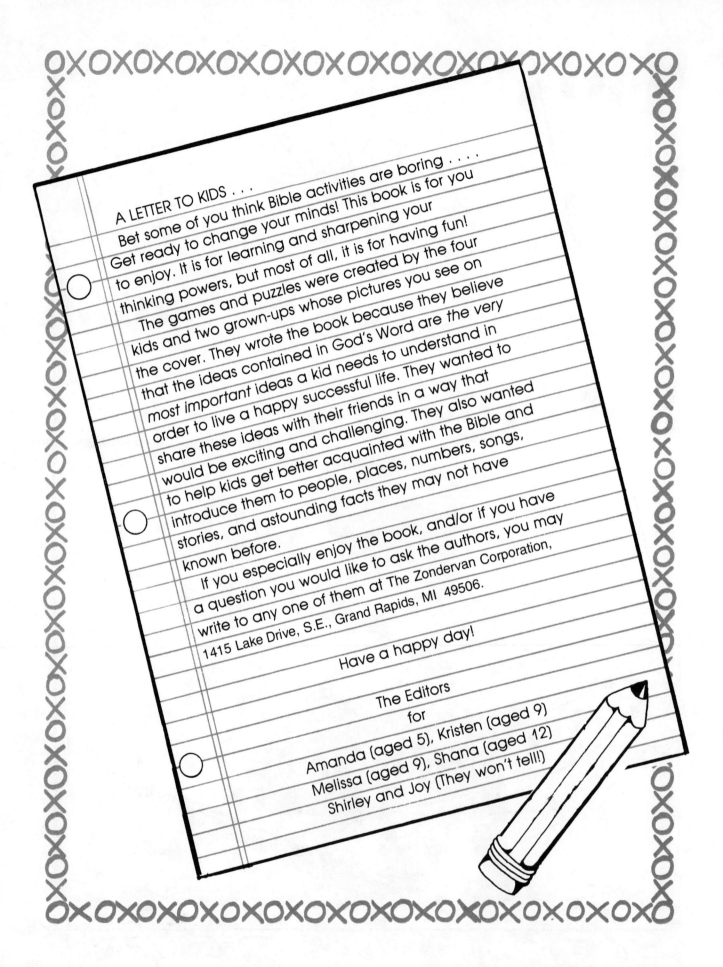

A LETTER TO KIDS . . .

Bet some of you think Bible activities are boring . . . . Get ready to change your minds! This book is for you to enjoy. It is for learning and sharpening your thinking powers, but most of all, it is for having fun!

The games and puzzles were created by the four kids and two grown-ups whose pictures you see on the cover. They wrote the book because they believe that the ideas contained in God's Word are the very most important ideas a kid needs to understand in order to live a happy successful life. They wanted to share these ideas with their friends in a way that would be exciting and challenging. They also wanted to help kids get better acquainted with the Bible and introduce them to people, places, numbers, songs, stories, and astounding facts they may not have known before.

If you especially enjoy the book, and/or if you have a question you would like to ask the authors, you may write to any one of them at The Zondervan Corporation, 1415 Lake Drive, S.E., Grand Rapids, MI 49506.

Have a happy day!

The Editors
for
Amanda (aged 5), Kristen (aged 9)
Melissa (aged 9), Shana (aged 12)
Shirley and Joy (They won't tell!)

4

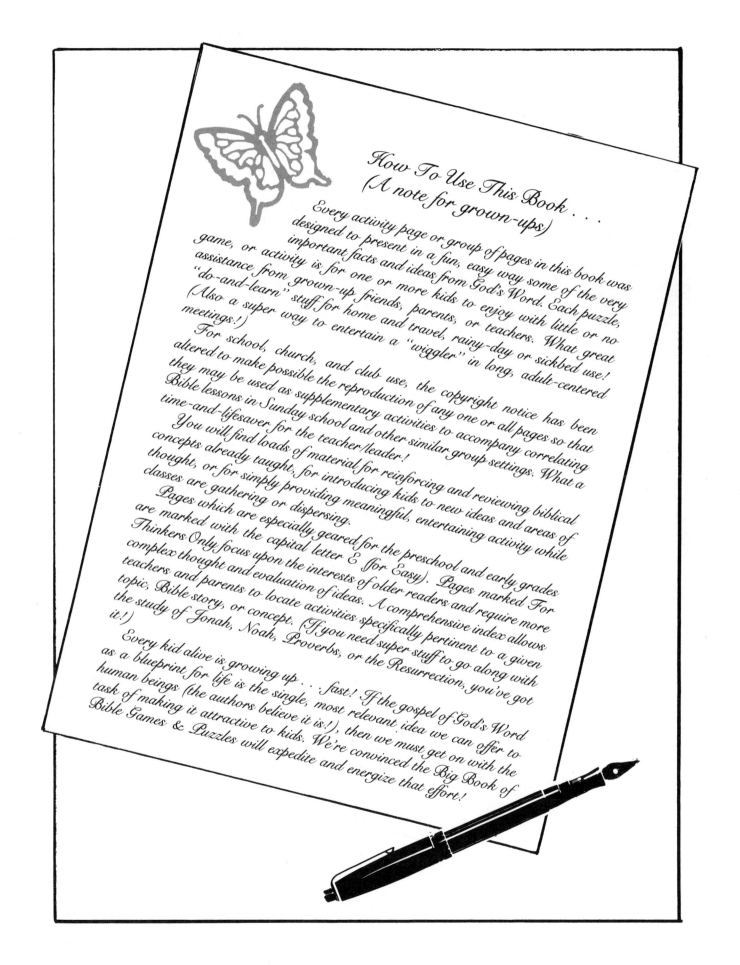

How To Use This Book . . .
(A note for grown-ups)

Every activity page or group of pages in this book was designed to present in a fun, easy way some of the very important facts and ideas from God's Word. Each puzzle, game, or activity is for one or more kids to enjoy with little or no assistance from grown-up friends, parents, or teachers. What great "do-and-learn" stuff for home and travel, rainy-day or sickbed use! (Also a super way to entertain a "wiggler" in long, adult-centered meetings!)

For school, church, and club use, the copyright notice has been altered to make possible the reproduction of any one or all pages so that they may be used as supplementary activities to accompany correlating Bible lessons in Sunday school and other similar group settings. What a time-and-lifesaver for the teacher/leader!

You will find loads of material for reinforcing and reviewing biblical concepts already taught, for introducing kids to new ideas and areas of thought, or for simply providing meaningful, entertaining activity while classes are gathering or dispersing.

Pages which are especially geared for the preschool and early grades are marked with the capital letter E (for Easy). Pages marked For Thinkers Only focus upon the interests of older readers and require more complex thought and evaluation of ideas. A comprehensive index allows teachers and parents to locate activities specifically pertinent to a given topic, Bible story, or concept. (If you need super stuff to go along with the study of Jonah, Noah, Proverbs, or the Resurrection, you've got it!)

Every kid alive is growing up . . . fast! If the gospel of God's Word as a blueprint for life is the single, most relevant idea we can offer to human beings (the authors believe it is!), then we must get on with the task of making it attractive to kids. We're convinced the Big Book of Bible Games & Puzzles will expedite and energize that effort!

Table of Contents

SCOOTER, DO YOU KNOW WHAT A TABLE OF CONTENTS IS ???

YUP! IT'S WHAT'S IN THIS BIG BOOK!

UH... DOESN'T SOUND LIKE THERE ARE GOING TO BE ANY TABLE SCRAPS!

THE WORLD'S BIGGEST BELLYACHE

Fill in the puzzle by reading the story below. (If you have trouble with the answers, you can find them in the first three chapters of the Book of Jonah.)

God told Jonah to go to 1 across _____ .
Instead, he got on a 6 across _____
and headed for 4 down _____ .
He was running away from 7 across _____ .
God caused a great 5 down _____ to come.
The sailors threw Jonah into the 3 down _____ . He was
swallowed by a great 2 down _____ .

Jonah was inside the animal 8 across _____ days and nights.
What a bellyache Jonah was! The fish felt so bad that he
vomited Jonah up on the sand. Yuk! Then Jonah obeyed God
and went on to Nineveh.

9

DANIEL'S SECRET WEAPON

Lions like this one waited for Daniel in the lions' den. But Daniel had a secret weapon that kept them from tearing him apart. He did something regularly that was obedient to God, and God honored Daniel for that faithful act and closed the lions' mouths. What did Daniel do so faithfully? The answer has four letters which are hidden in this picture. Find them and write them on the line below.

Answer: ____ ____ ____ ____

the CAREER CONNECTION

See if you can match these Bible characters with their chosen careers or jobs. (Choose the BEST match for each one . . . careful — it's tricky!)

Joseph	Tax collector
Luke	Magician
Jehu	Fisherman
Peter	Queen
Nicodemus	Carpenter
Caleb	Prime Minister
Solomon	Beggar
Simon	Chariot Driver
David (boy)	A Good Wife
Matthew & Zacchaeus	Soldier
Jeremiah	King
Aquila	Doctor
Gideon	Prophet
Bartimaeus	Shepherd
Deborah	Judge
Jezebel	Tentmaker
Abigail	Spy
Haman	Rabbi

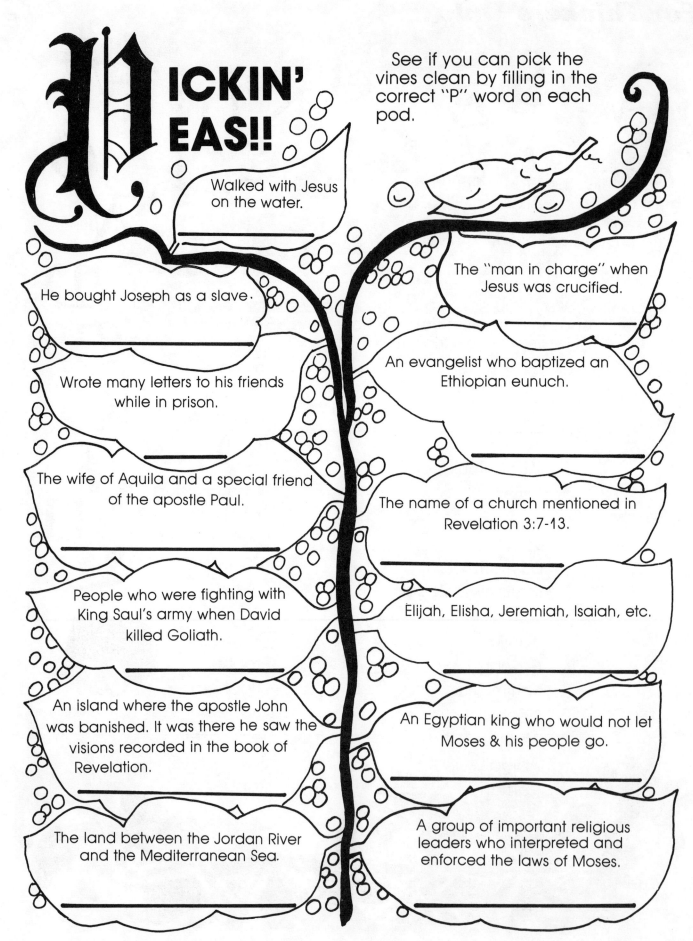

PICKIN' PEAS!!

See if you can pick the vines clean by filling in the correct "P" word on each pod.

Walked with Jesus on the water.

_____

The "man in charge" when Jesus was crucified.

_____

He bought Joseph as a slave.

_____

An evangelist who baptized an Ethiopian eunuch.

_____

Wrote many letters to his friends while in prison.

_____

The name of a church mentioned in Revelation 3:7-13.

_____

The wife of Aquila and a special friend of the apostle Paul.

_____

Elijah, Elisha, Jeremiah, Isaiah, etc.

_____

People who were fighting with King Saul's army when David killed Goliath.

_____

An island where the apostle John was banished. It was there he saw the visions recorded in the book of Revelation.

_____

An Egyptian king who would not let Moses & his people go.

_____

The land between the Jordan River and the Mediterranean Sea.

_____

A group of important religious leaders who interpreted and enforced the laws of Moses.

_____

For Thinkers Only ...

WISE AND WONDERFUL

Wise Willy, the Wonderful Worm, knows all the answers. You must ask the questions.

The words at the left are Wise Willy's answers. On each line, write a question for which his answer will be correct.

1. salt _____?

2. a rainbow _____?

3. angels _____?

4. Joash _____?

5. a chariot _____?

6. a donkey _____?

7. a cave _____?

8. a tower _____?

9. a wall _____?

10. a silver cup _____?

11. a coin (or coins) _____?

12. Naomi _____?

13

ANIMAL ACROSTIC

camel

sheep

wolf

bee

horse

lizard

lion

lamb

bear

snake

locust

donkey

**B
I
B
L
E

A
N
I
M
A
L
S**

The Bible mentions over 130 animals. These are just a few of them. See if you can complete the acrostic by writing each animal name in its proper "across" spaces.

14

CASE OF THE LURKING LETTER

The letters below form one sentence, but there is one naughty letter which "lurks" in between the other letters to mess up the message. Find the "lurking letter" and cross it out, wherever you find it. Then you will be able to read the hidden sentence. Write it on the lines below.

A V E C R C Y I M C P O R T C A N C T

B O C O K I S C G O D'S C H O L C Y W

O R C D, T C H E B I C B L E.

_____

_____

_____

CRACK THE CODE

Break the code and you will find a promise from Jesus for those who are persistent in their prayers. You can read this promise in Luke 11:10 TLB.

A	C	D
E	F	H
I	K	L

N	O	P
R	S	T
V	W	Y

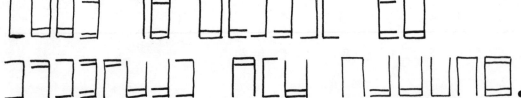

Write your decoded message here:

_____

_____

_____

_____

The home pictured here is similar to the home into which Jesus was (E) born. Study the picture for a couple of minutes. Then turn to the next page, and answer the questions to see how much you can remember about it.

You might like to challenge a friend to test his memory along with you.

Home Sweet Home

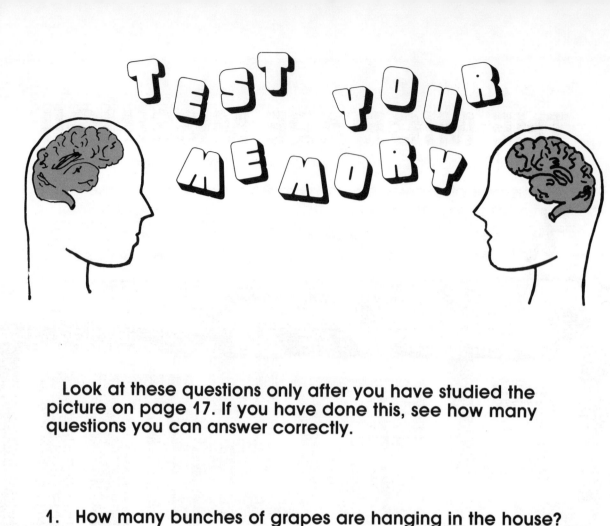

TEST YOUR MEMORY

Look at these questions only after you have studied the picture on page 17. If you have done this, see how many questions you can answer correctly.

1. How many bunches of grapes are hanging in the house?
2. What is on the windowsill?
3. What did you see outside the window?
4. How many chickens are inside the house?
5. How many sheep are inside the house?
6. What other animals are inside?
7. What did you see outside the door?
8. What is in the vase behind the door?
9. What is next to the door?
10. How many folded bedrolls are on the floor?
11. Is the man in the picture sitting or standing?
12. Does he have shoes on or is he barefoot?
13. What is cooking on the small stove?

If you answered 8 or more questions correctly, give your memory a great big smily face here: ◯

THE MICE ARE MISSING!!

This pair of mice has been chosen by Noah to join the animals in the ark, but they have wandered off for one last juicy meal, and now they are lost!! Help them get back to the ark.

A *BALD* HEAD IS BETTER

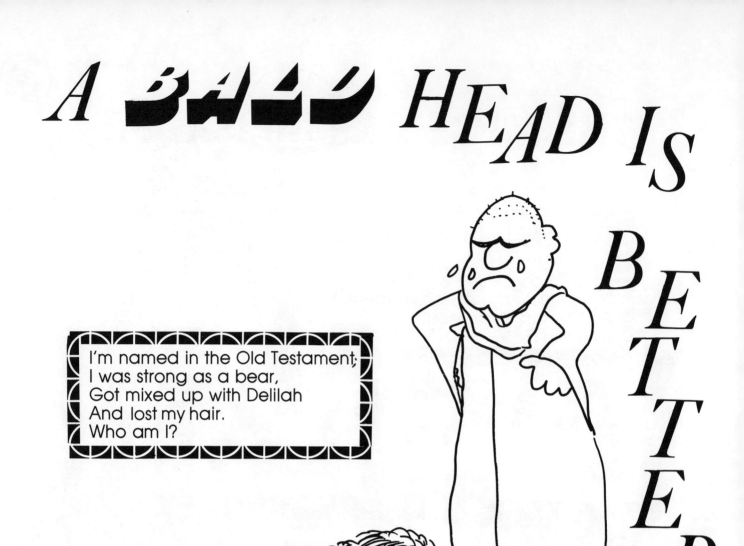

I'm named in the Old Testament;
I was strong as a bear,
Got mixed up with Delilah
And lost my hair.
Who am I?

The birthright went to the first born;
That was the Jewish law,
I bought it for a bowl of soup
From my brother — my twin, Esau
Who am I?

I said, "She's a bad queen!"
And her anger grew red.
So she tricked husband Herod
And he cut off my head.
Who am I?

THAN NO HEAD AT ALL

I had Christians killed;
They hated me,
I had to be blinded
Before I could see.
Who am I?

LEAPIN' LIZARDS

Can you imagine living in a town where all the water is blood or where all the animals are dying of a terrible disease? How would you like living with thousands of frogs or lizards leaping all over you? It would be very difficult to eat or sleep or even think with flies or lice or locusts crawling about. That's the way it was in Egypt for awhile. Read Exodus 7:14 - 10:29 to find out why. Then look at the group of words on each lizard.

Hidden somewhere in each group of words is the name of one of the ten plagues God brought to Pharoah's people. Write the correct plague (listed on page 23) on each lizard's tail.

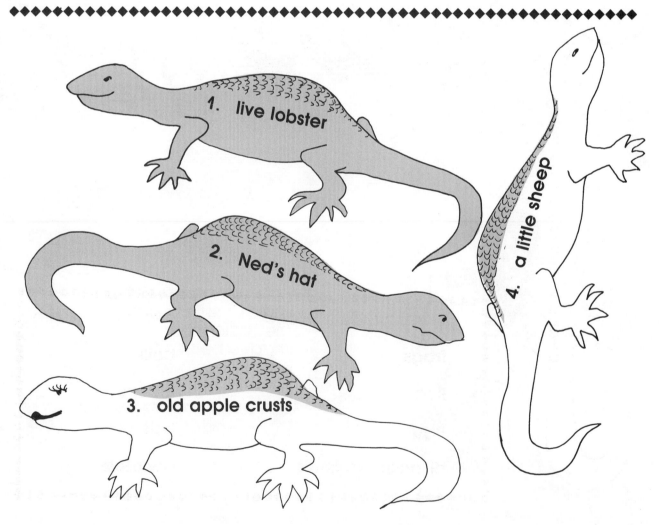

1. live lobster

2. Ned's hat

3. old apple crusts

4. a little sheep

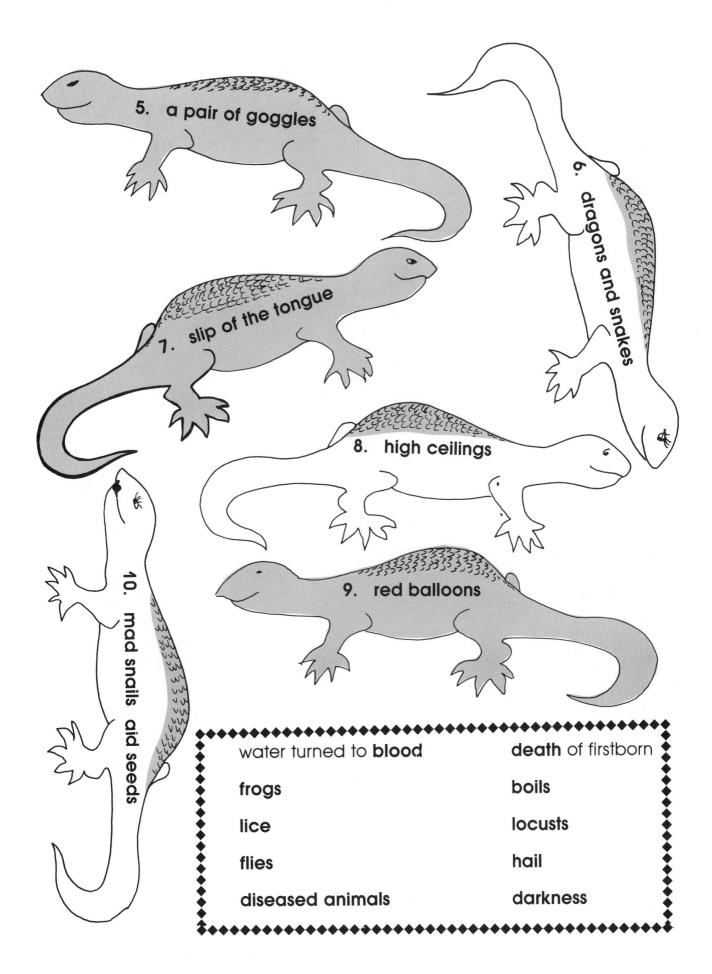

5. a pair of goggles

6. dragons and snakes

7. slip of the tongue

8. high ceilings

9. red balloons

10. mad snails aid seeds

water turned to **blood**	**death** of firstborn
frogs	boils
lice	locusts
flies	hail
diseased animals	darkness

CLOTHESLINE

1. How many pictures show stories about a special boy? _____
2. How many pictures show people who obeyed God? _____
3. How many pictures show people whom God saved from death or tragedy? _____
4. How many pictures show people to whom God made special promises? _____
5. How many pictures show stories about a dream? _____
6. How many pictures show people who disobeyed God? _____

COUNTDOWN

Write on each picture the name of at least one person you see in the picture.

If the numbers you have written total 12 or MORE, you are a very good thinker. Give yourself an A+!

...COMPARABLE

Billy was on his way to school when his pant leg got caught in his bicycle chain. He couldn't ride any farther. He couldn't even get loose from the bike. His best friend came along, but said he couldn't stop, for it would make him late to class. His next door neighbor rode past him, but pretended he didn't see him. Then a girl whom he did not know at all came by. She was hurrying to finish her paper route, but she saw his problem and helped him get free from the bicycle. She even took time to pick up some books he had dropped.

A parable is a story from which a lesson can be learned. Jesus told many parables to help people understand his teachings.

Here are some modern parables. Each is like one that Jesus told. Can you write the name of the famous parable that teaches the same lesson as each of these?

Mary and Elaine were talking when, suddenly, Mary got her feelings hurt over something Elaine said and left abruptly. Elaine was surprised. Elaine talked to other friends about what had happened. They told her not to worry about it because she had at least ninety-nine other friends and she wouldn't even miss Mary. But Elaine liked Mary and did not want to lose her friendship. She asked Mary to talk to her about the misunderstanding. Mary was glad to know Elaine didn't mean to hurt her feelings. She apologized for getting angry too quickly. Elaine was happy that she did not lose Mary as a friend.

PARABLES......

Cathy and Bob wanted to build a cardboard fort to play in. Bob's mother suggested they place it at the bottom of the hill on the side of the house that was protected from the wind. Bob and Cathy insisted on putting it at the top of the hill on the other side of the house. After all, the wind didn't seem to be blowing anyway. By the time they finished building the fort, it was dark. They had to quit for the day. When they got back to the fort the next morning, the cardboard had been scattered by the wind during the night.

Choose another Bible parable from this list or pick one that is your favorite. Write your own "updated" version.

Weeds Among the Wheat (Matthew 13:24-30)
The Unmerciful Servant (Matthew 18:23-35)
The Wise and Foolish Maidens (Matthew 25:1-13)
Lamp Under a Bushel (Mark 4:21-22)
The Prodigal Son (Luke 15:11-32)

For Thinkers Only ...

FAMOUS

The Bible tells many intriguing stories about people who designed deceitful tricks and fakes. Often, these deeds were a matter of life and death. Make all these sentences true by choosing one word or phrase from the list to fill in each space. Use each word only once.

1. _____' mother hid him in a tiny ark of _____ . (Exodus 2:3)

2. David's _____ put a statue in his _____ and helped him escape through a _____ . (I Samuel 19:11-14)

3. _____ settled an argument between two _____ by threatening to cut a _____ in half. (I Kings 3:17-28)

4. _____'s friends helped him escape over a _____ at night in a _____ . (Acts 9:23-25)

5. _____ impersonated his brother, _____ to trick his father, _____ into giving him his brother's birthright. (Genesis 27:1-29)

FAKES

& TRICKS...

28

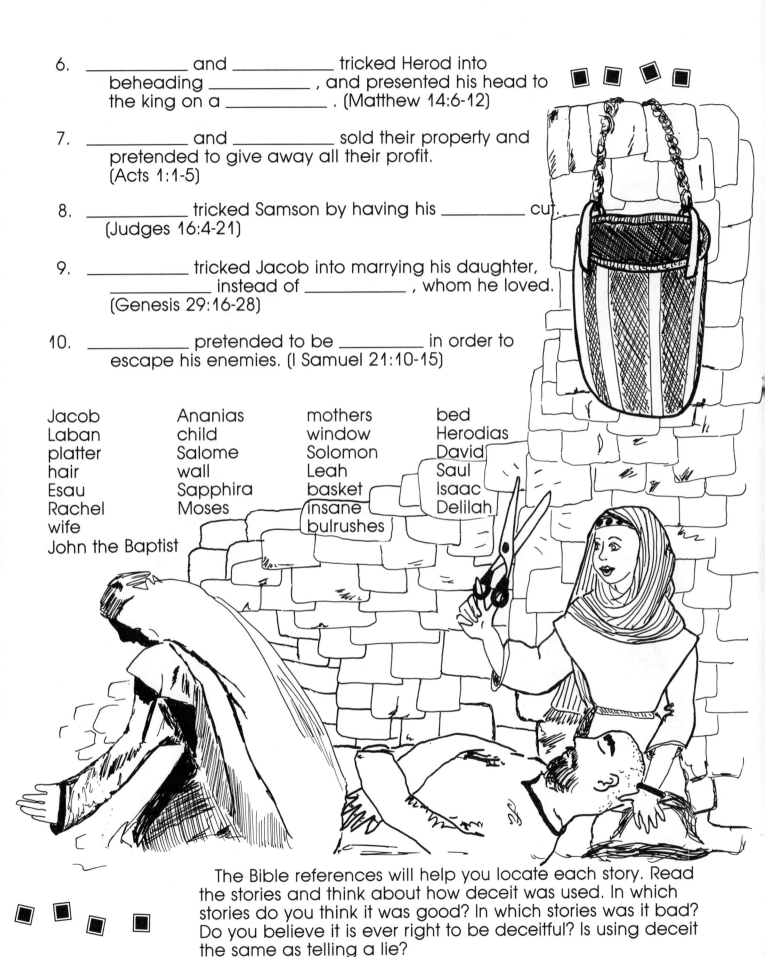

6. _____ and _____ tricked Herod into beheading _____ , and presented his head to the king on a _____ . (Matthew 14:6-12)

7. _____ and _____ sold their property and pretended to give away all their profit. (Acts 1:1-5)

8. _____ tricked Samson by having his _____ cut. (Judges 16:4-21)

9. _____ tricked Jacob into marrying his daughter, _____ instead of _____ , whom he loved. (Genesis 29:16-28)

10. _____ pretended to be _____ in order to escape his enemies. (I Samuel 21:10-15)

Jacob	Ananias	mothers	bed
Laban	child	window	Herodias
platter	Salome	Solomon	David
hair	wall	Leah	Saul
Esau	Sapphira	basket	Isaac
Rachel	Moses	insane	Delilah
wife		bulrushes	
John the Baptist			

The Bible references will help you locate each story. Read the stories and think about how deceit was used. In which stories do you think it was good? In which stories was it bad? Do you believe it is ever right to be deceitful? Is using deceit the same as telling a lie?

MIXED MATCH

Each picture on this page goes with one of the pictures on the opposite page. Draw lines to match the pictures that belong together.

See how many of these stories you can retell in your very own words.

For Thinkers Only ...

JUST THE

You're going to need your thinking cap and. . .

DOWN

1. Made ready (I Corinthians. 2:9).
3. Not dark (Matthew 5:16).
4. A large bird which is the U.S. symbol (Proverbs 23:5).
5. To take something that does not belong to you (Exodus 20:15).
6. Water falling from clouds (Genesis 7:12).
7. Being useful to others (John 16:2).
8. Shape (Genesis 1:2).
12. Condition of being friends (Proverbs 22:24).
13. To worship or praise (Psalms 86:9).
15. No flaws (Luke 6:40).
17. Opposite of south (Psalms 107:3).
19. Lasting for all time (Deuteronomy 33:27).
22. A fond, deep, tender feeling (Matthew 5:44).
24. Part of the body with which one sees (Matthew 18:9).

ACROSS

2. Quality of behaving justly (Psalms 4:1).
9. Opposite of a friend (James 4:4).
10. The leader of a state (Psalms 22:28).
11. A shelter from danger or trouble (Psalms 14:6).
14. One who sins (James 4:8).
16. Act of obeying (Romans 1:5).
18. Flame (Genesis 22:7).
20. A fellow human being (As spelled in Matthew 5:43, KJV).
21. Our heavenly Father (Matthew 1:23).
23. Written on stationery (II Corinthians 3:6).
25. To give in to (Psalms 107:37).
26. Kind of plant on which grapes grow (John 15:1).
27. To make well (Psalms 41:4).
28. To worship in words or songs (Psalms 148:1).

RIGHT WORD!

. . . . . .a King James Bible for this one!

TAG the TOE

Look carefully at each pair of feet. To which person listed below might each pair belong? Write the correct name on each toe tag!

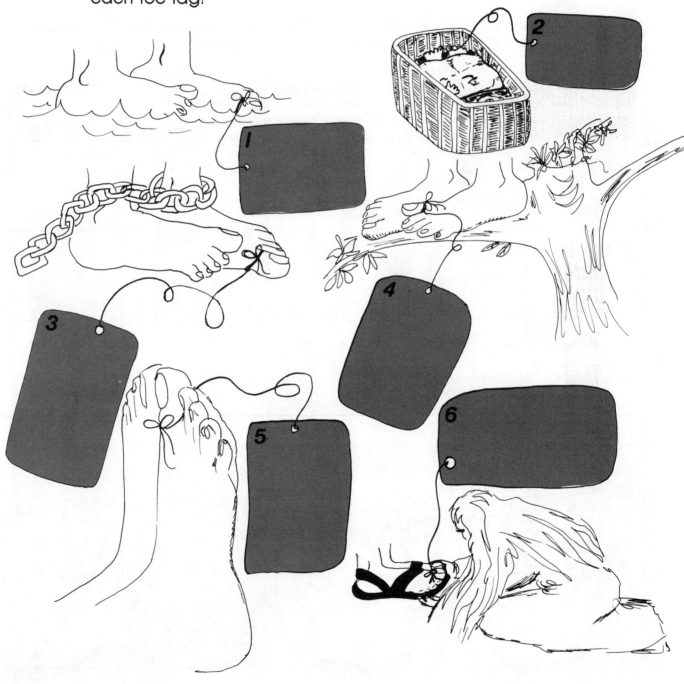

Peter   **Paul**   **Zacchaeus**   **Goliath**   **Moses**   **Jesus**

FACTS in FOURS

Fill in each space with an item that fits the category above and begins with the letter to the left.

	ACTIONS THAT DISPLEASE GOD	NEW TESTAMENT BOOKS	ACTIONS THAT PLEASE GOD	OLD TESTAMENT BOOKS
J				
M				
H				
P				

THE PATH FINDER

Proverbs 2:20 tells us to follow those who set a good example. Help the young girl find the "right" path through this letter maze by drawing one continuous line through the letters of this verse from Proverbs: **"Follow the steps of the godly . . . and stay on the right path" (TLB).**

Now read the verse two or three times and try to write it without looking at it.

_____

_____

_____

_____

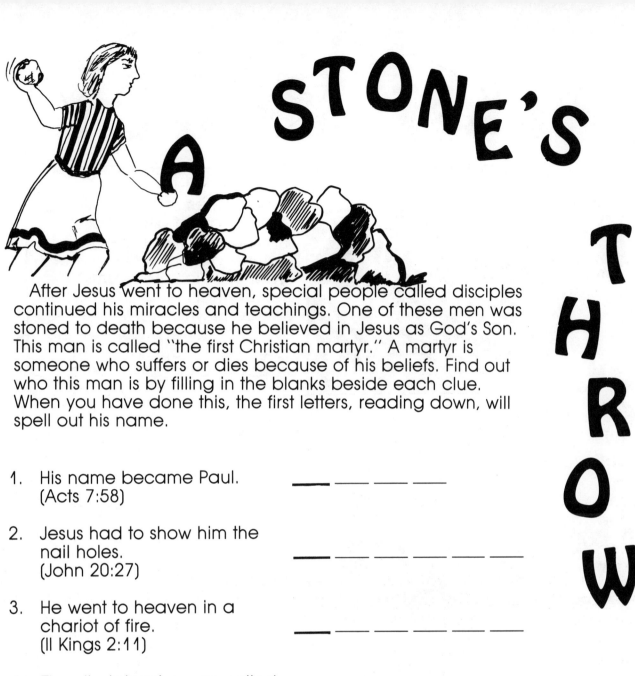

A STONE'S THROW

After Jesus went to heaven, special people called disciples continued his miracles and teachings. One of these men was stoned to death because he believed in Jesus as God's Son. This man is called "the first Christian martyr." A martyr is someone who suffers or dies because of his beliefs. Find out who this man is by filling in the blanks beside each clue. When you have done this, the first letters, reading down, will spell out his name.

1. His name became Paul. (Acts 7:58)

    ＿ ＿ ＿ ＿

2. Jesus had to show him the nail holes. (John 20:27)

    ＿ ＿ ＿ ＿ ＿ ＿

3. He went to heaven in a chariot of fire. (II Kings 2:11)

    ＿ ＿ ＿ ＿ ＿

4. The disciple who was called "the rock." (Matthew 16:18)

    ＿ ＿ ＿ ＿ ＿

5. She was the mother of Samuel. (I Samuel 1:20)

    ＿ ＿ ＿ ＿ ＿

6. He was the priest who taught Samuel. (I Samuel 1:25)

    ＿ ＿ ＿

7. He was a soldier who was cured of leprosy. (II Kings 5)

    ＿ ＿ ＿ ＿ ＿

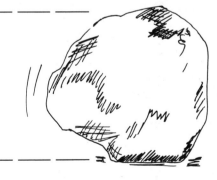

Aren't we glad we can be Christians without fear for our lives?

FILM FANCY

(E)

The frames on this filmstrip tell the story of one of Jesus' miracles. However, the pictures are not shown in the order in which the events actually happened. Can you decide in what order the events occurred? Number the pictures, 1 through 5, in the small circle on each frame.

1.

You can read this story in Matthew 9:2-8.

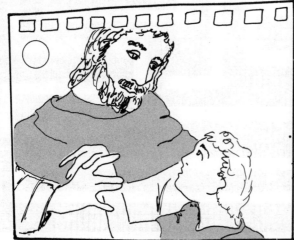

A TREE FOR ZACH

Zacchaeus is such a short man, and he is so curious about Jesus. Help him find a sycamore tree he can climb so he can see and hear Jesus.

a timed test

Using the letters in the top of the hourglass, time yourself to see how long it takes to complete the names of the first twelve disciples. The letters may be used more than once. You can find help in Mark 3:16-19.

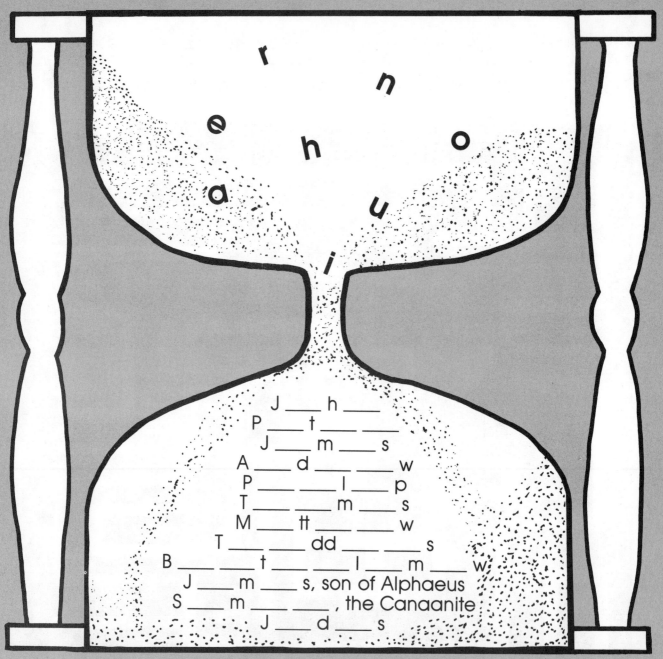

If you completed the twelve names correctly in less than five minutes, consider yourself an expert. If you can write all twelve names on another sheet of paper, without looking back to this page, consider yourself a "super-duper" expert.

Each name of a Bible personality rhymes with the name of something pictured below. Write the rhyming word in the space beside the name.

Moses _____   Job _____

James _____   Mark _____

Mary _____   Paul _____

Lot _____   Peter _____

Ruth _____   Cain _____

A REBUS RHYME

41

GUESS WHO'S IN THE BUSHES!

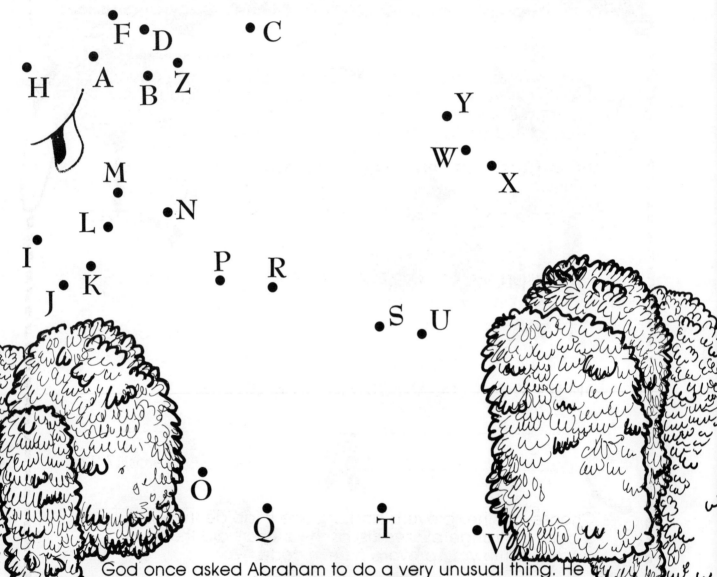

God once asked Abraham to do a very unusual thing. He asked him to tie his only son, Isaac, to an altar and kill him. God was testing Abraham to see if he would really obey and trust God. Abraham did exactly as God told him. But as he raised his knife to kill Isaac, God showed him something that was caught in the bushes nearby. Abraham could use this in place of Isaac for a sacrifice to God.

Connect the dots to find out what God gave to Abraham.

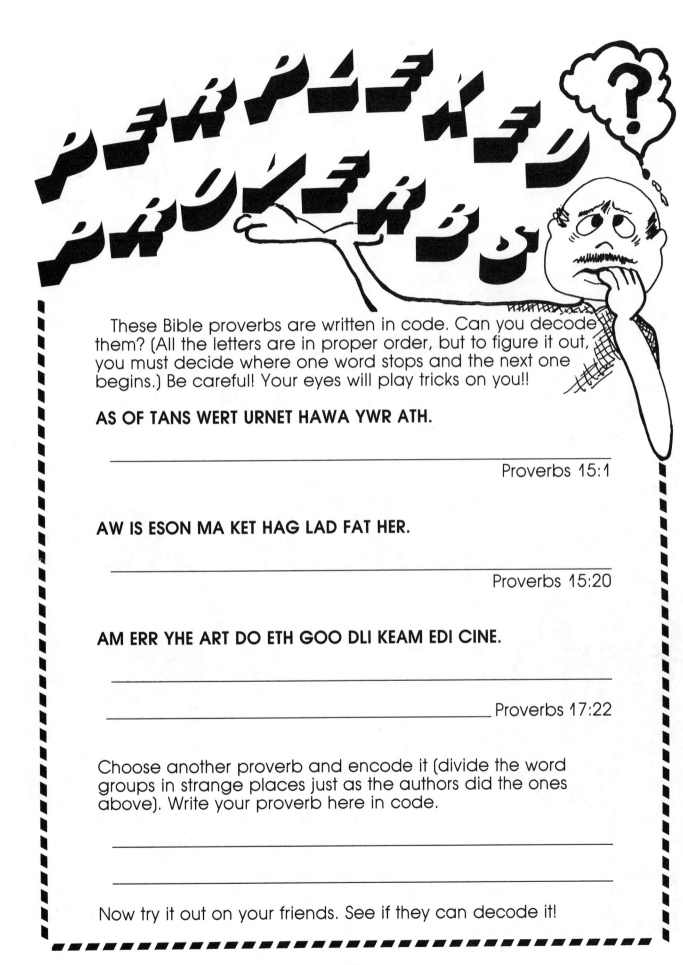

PERPLEXED PROVERBS

These Bible proverbs are written in code. Can you decode them? (All the letters are in proper order, but to figure it out, you must decide where one word stops and the next one begins.) Be careful! Your eyes will play tricks on you!!

AS OF TANS WERT URNET HAWA YWR ATH.

_____

Proverbs 15:1

AW IS ESON MA KET HAG LAD FAT HER.

_____

Proverbs 15:20

AM ERR YHE ART DO ETH GOO DLI KEAM EDI CINE.

_____

_____ Proverbs 17:22

Choose another proverb and encode it (divide the word groups in strange places just as the authors did the ones above). Write your proverb here in code.

_____

_____

Now try it out on your friends. See if they can decode it!

43

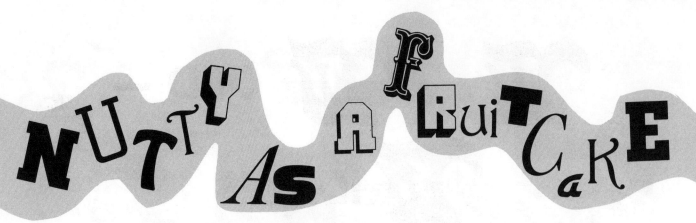

NUTTY AS A FRUITCAKE

In this fruitcake, you will find 12 ingredients a good cook of Bible times might have used. See if you can unscramble the letters to discover what's in the cake. Write your answers along the edge of the plate.

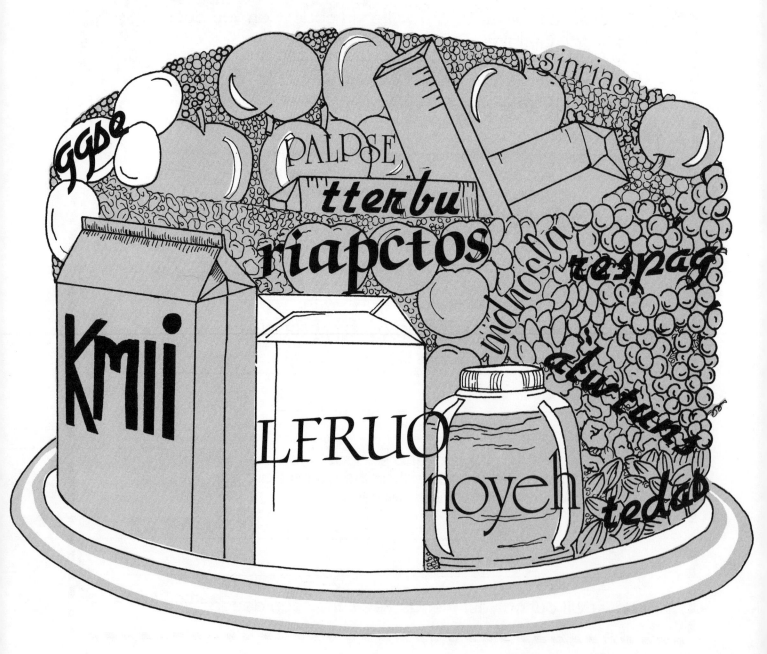

W – WORD – WIDDLES

Find the words described, letter by letter. Then write each word in a verse at the bottom of the page.

1. My first letter is in **word** and also in **want**,
   My second letter is in **wore** but not in **wire**,
   My third letter is in **write** but not in **white**,
   My fourth letter is in **whisk** but not in **whish**.

   ___ ___ ___ ___

2. My first letter is in **wood** and also in **wealth**,
   My second letter is in **water** but not in **writer**,
   My third letter is in **while** but not in **whale**,
   My fourth letter is in **went** but not in **when**.

   ___ ___ ___ ___

3. My first letter is in **wear** and also in **wool**,
   My second letter is in **wind** but not in **wand**,
   My third letter is in **wish** but not in **with**,
   My fourth letter is in **wind** but not in **wing**,
   My fifth letter is in **won** but not in **win**,
   My sixth letter is in **worm** but not in **worn**.

   ___ ___ ___ ___ ___ ___

Verses from Proverbs:

1. " ___ ___ ___ ___ of the godly will flourish."
   (Proverbs 14:11)

2. "Don't repay evil for evil. ___ ___ ___ ___ for the Lord to handle the matter."(Proverbs 20:22)

3. " ___ ___ ___ ___ ___ ___ is mightier than strength."
   (Proverbs 24:5)

45

BiBLE superlatives

Use the list of names below to fill in the
FIRST — LAST — BEST — WORST — MOST — ETC. stuff
on this page.

1. First man _____
2. Oldest man _____
3. The book with the fewest number of verses _____
4. Probably the strongest man in the Bible _____
5. Probably the tallest man in the Bible (over 9 ft.) _____
6. One of the shortest men in the Bible _____
7. Wrote the most books in the Bible (13 or 14) _____
8. Israel's first king _____
9. Jesus' first miracle _____
10. First Gentile to become a Christian _____
11. Man who wrote the most songs in the Bible _____
12. First book in the Bible _____
13. First murderer _____
14. The last book in the Bible _____
15. One of Israel's meanest kings _____
16. One of Israel's kindest kings _____
17. World's best-selling book _____
18. One of the Bible's wickedest grandmothers _____

Genesis	Methuselah	Water to wine	2 John
Solomon	Cain	King Saul	Samson
Manasseh	King David	Paul	Revelation
Adam	Cornelius	Zacchaeus	Goliath
	Bible	Athaliah	

the way to heaven

X CEPT A [man] [bee] BORN AGAIN, he [can] [worm] [sea] the [king]-dumb of GOD.

n 3:3

Write the verse here in words.

_____

_____

_____

Now repeat it to yourself five times. Then try to say it without looking. If you have said it perfectly, shake your hand and give yourself a pat on the back. Then draw a smily face here.

47

Put-Together Parts

If you can draw a line to connect each item in Column I
with the correct matches in Columns II and III, you will
complete 12 true sentences. (Warning: It "ain't" easy!)

I	II	III
1. Noah	was Jesus' friend	from prison.
2. Lazarus	destroyed a prison	to see whose God was real.
3. Jehu	led a march	at night.
4. Angels	commanded some men	and increased her food supply.
5. Nicodemus	rescued Peter	and a family found God.
6. A widow	built a boat	between two mothers.
7. Naaman	fed Elijah	who rose from the dead.
8. Elijah	came to see Jesus	to throw a queen out a window.
9. A wise king	was awakened in the night	even though people laughed.
10. Joshua	settled a fight	and was healed of leprosy.
11. Samuel	had a contest with the prophets of Baal	around a wall.
12. An earthquake	dipped seven times in a river	by a voice calling.

MIDNIGHT VISITOR

Each blank space on this page represents a missing consonant. See if you can fill every space with the proper letter. Then read the story and follow the instructions. (You may want to read John 3:1-16 to get help with your answer.)

A ve ___ y im ___ o ___ ta ___ ___ ma ___

ca ___ e ___ o Je ___ u ___ o ___ e ___ i ___ ht.

___ e ___ a ___ e a ___ ___ igh ___

___ e ___ au ___ s he ___ i ___ n' ___ ___ a ___ t

___ is f ___ ie ___ ds ___ o ___ ee ___ im.

___ e ___ us ___ ol ___ ___ im

___ o ___ ethi ___ ___ st ___ a ___ ge.

Je ___ u ___ ___ ai ___ , "You ___ u ___ t ___ e

bo ___ n a ___ ai ___ !"

T ___ e ma ___ 's ___ ame ___ as

Ni ___ o ___ emu ___ .

Can you explain what Jesus meant?

Write your explanation here.

_____

_____

_____

For Thinkers Only ...

49

NO LIES— THAT'S WISE!

Mark the sentences true **(T)** or false **(F)**. After checking your answers, change one word in each false sentence that will make it true. Circle the word you are changing, and write the new word at the end of the sentence.

__ 1. Jesus was born in a hospital. _____

__ 2. Daniel was put in a den full of tigers. _____

__ 3. Adam was the first man God made. _____

__ 4. Joseph's father, Jacob, gave him a special coat of many colors. _____

__ 5. Jonah was swallowed by a large turtle. _____

__ 6. The wise men found baby Jesus by following a star. _____

__ 7. God gave the Ten Commandments to Daniel. _____

__ 8. Samson was a weak man. _____

__ 9. Goliath died in a fight with a girl. _____

__ 10. Noah and his family survived a great fire. _____

__ 11. Zacchaeus was able to see Jesus by climbing a pole. _____

__ 12. Jesus was able to walk on water. _____

50

PUT CHRIST FIRST IN YOUR LIFE

Jesus said, "I am the way, the truth, and the life" (John 14:16). He wants and even expects us to keep Him involved in all our activities.

Fill in the squares under each letter in CHRIST by using these clues:

C — where you worship on Sunday.

H — where you sleep, and eat, and watch T V.

R — playtime at school.

I — a word that describes you when you are doing nothing.

S — where you study, learn, and play.

T — what you do when you go on a trip.

C	H	R	I	S	T

CHARACTER COMPOSITE

For Thinkers Only ...

Choose one name from the list below. Write it in the center circle. Read the labels around the outside of the square. In each space, write at least one phrase or sentence that tells something about that category in the life of the person whose name appears in the circle.

Esau	Paul	Peter	Timothy	Ruth
Joseph	John the Baptist	Esther	Elijah	Daniel

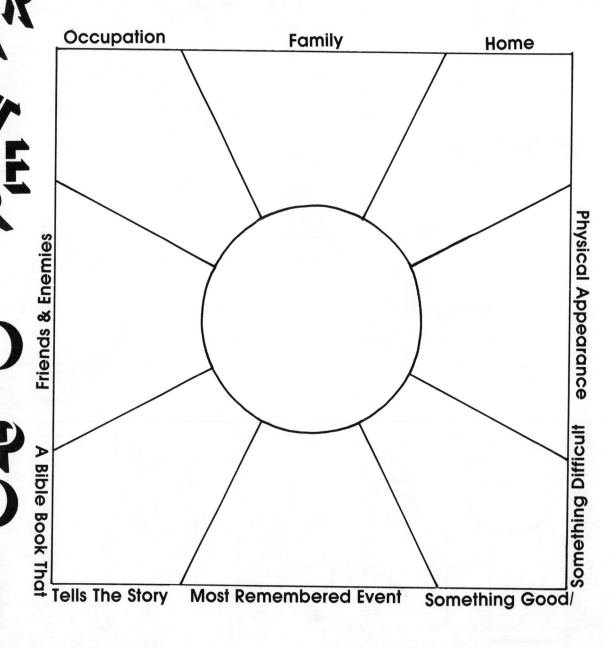

Occupation   **Family**   **Home**

Friends & Enemies

A Bible Book That

Physical Appearance

Something Difficult

Tells The Story   **Most Remembered Event**   **Something Good/**

Note: You might trace the lines of this chart on your own paper and make more "character composites," using names you choose. You might even keep a special notebook on Bible characters you study in this way.

NOW & Then

Draw a line to match each "today" picture with a "Bible-time" picture.

Read up, down, forward, backward, or diagonally to find the names of these Bible prophets.

Malachi	Elijah	Micah	Zechariah
Obadiah	Amos	Elisha	Isaiah
Joel	Jonah	Jeremiah	Zephaniah
Habakkuk	Haggai	Hosea	Nahum

poem people

A male In a whale	Saul
In a bed Overhead	Joshua
A goat On a boat	Noah
A mighty sling For a future king	Jonah
A light That blinds sight	a lame man
Something sweet On feet	Zacchaeus
The fall Of a wall	Mary of Bethany
A "he" In a tree	David

Read these short rhymes. Then match poems and people by drawing a line to connect each poem to the correct person.

FACE UP!

Put an **X** on the face that tells how Herod felt when the wise men did not return.

Circle the face that shows how God feels when we tell a lie.

Make a **squiggly line** through the face that shows how Sarah felt when she first learned she was going to have Isaac.

Make a **square box** around the face that shows how the shepherds felt when they first saw the angel who announced Jesus' birth.

Make a **halo over** the face that shows how Mary Magdalene felt when she went to the tomb on Easter morning and found it empty.

RAIN-EE DAY

If you let the 13 E's fall down into the Bible verse in the right places, you will find a message that will help you turn all your rainy days into happy days.

E E E E E
E E E
E E E E E
E

"W H N A M A N I S G L O O M Y , V R Y T H I N G S M S T O
G O W R O N G ; W H N H I S C H R F U L , V R Y T H I N G S M S
R I G H T."

Proverbs 15:15 TLB

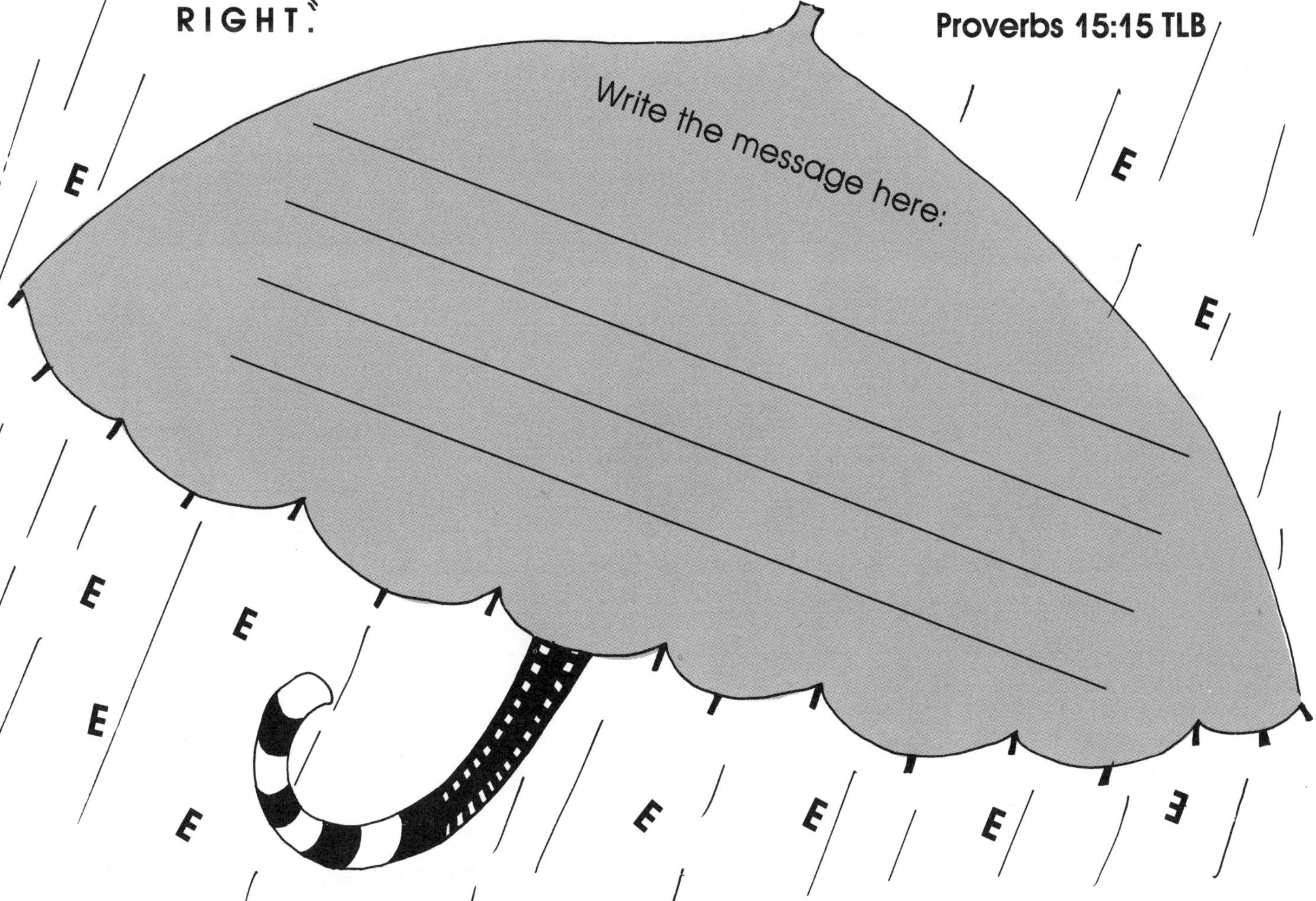

Write the message here:

_____

_____

_____

_____

E E E E E E
E E E E

It All Started With The Creation

Aren't we glad God felt like inventing that week? We should say "Thank You!" to Him every day for all the beautiful things He made. Do a little creating of your own and see how many words you can make using the letters in the word "CREATION". You might like to challenge a friend to a contest to see who can make the most words. There are at least 100 words!

CREATION

I'm glad I didn't have to make a whole world. Whew!

what a world!

This picture is for you to color and frame.
Make it beautiful . . . . . just as God made our world!

Sorry, wrong number!

In each sentence below, there is a number that makes the sentence false. Change the number to make it true. You can find the answer by looking up the scripture reference at the end of the sentence.

1. Jacob had 11 sons who founded the 12 tribes of Israel. (Genesis 35:22)

2. On Mt. Sinai, God gave Moses 8 Commandments for him to take down to the people. (Exodus 34:28)

3. Joshua, who led the Israelites after Moses died, sent 20 spies to Jericho to learn all they could about the city. (Joshua 2:1)

4. The shortest book of the Old Testament is Obadiah which has only 20 verses. (Obadiah)

5. Jesus was found by His parents teaching His elders in the temple at Jerusalem when He was only 15. (Luke 2:42)

6. By sharing 4 loaves of bread and 2 small fish, a young boy helped Jesus feed thousands of people. (Luke 6:9)

7. At the Last Supper, Jesus had his 18 disciples gathered around Him. (Matthew 26:14)

8. Judas betrayed Jesus with a kiss and was paid 200 pieces of silver. (Matthew 26:15)

9. Simon Peter denied he knew Jesus 2 times on the night of the arrest — just as Jesus had told him he would. (Matthew 26:75)

10. After Jesus arose from the dead on Easter Sunday, he stayed on earth for 25 days before He ascended into heaven. (Acts 1:3)

GIVE ME FIVE!

See if you can do this whole page of FIVES in just FIVE minutes.

Name 5 books of the Old Testament.

1. _____
2. _____
3. _____
4. _____
5. _____

Name 5 books of the New Testament.

1. _____
2. _____
3. _____
4. _____
5. _____

Give a five-letter answer to these riddles:

1. God's Son ___ ___ ___ ___ ___

2. Announced Jesus' birth ___ ___ ___ ___ ___

3. The world's most famous Book ___ ___ ___ ___ ___

4. Abraham is noted for his great ___ ___ ___ ___ ___ in God.

5. ___ ___ ___ ___ ___ from a special tree was forbidden to Adam & Eve.

Write the name of a Bible character whose name starts with each of these first FIVE letters of the alphabet.

A _____

B _____

C _____

D _____

E _____

61

A SAFE TRIP home

The good Samaritan helped a man who was not his friend. See if you can help this good man get all the way home without meeting any trouble!

TWIN BUTTERFLIES

The butterfly is a symbol of the Resurrection of Christ. It is one of God's loveliest creations. Show which butterflies are twins by coloring them exactly alike. Color the others a different color.

E

For Thinkers Only ...

Sometimes our hearts are like deep, dark caves. All kinds of bad feelings and habits hide there, like goblins in the night. Now and then, they get out and bother us. Read these Bible verses to find out what goblins might be hiding inside you. Write a name on each figure you see in the cave.

Ephesians 4:31   Ephesians 5:4   Colossians 3:8,9   I John 3:15

Use a black crayon to color them all away. Press hard with the crayon so that you won't be able to see the names of the figures of these bad goblins any more. That's just how Jesus takes our sins away and forgets them when we ask Him to. Pray and ask him to help you keep these bad habits and feelings out of your heart.

Now read I John 1:9 and write here what God says He will do when you ask Him to.

_____

_____

_____

grodna

1 _____

blma

2 _____

SILHOUETTE SCRAMBLE

Unscramble the letters below each silhouette to find the name of each Bible animal.

lacem

3 _____

pearlod

4 _____

niol

5 _____

For Thinkers Only ...

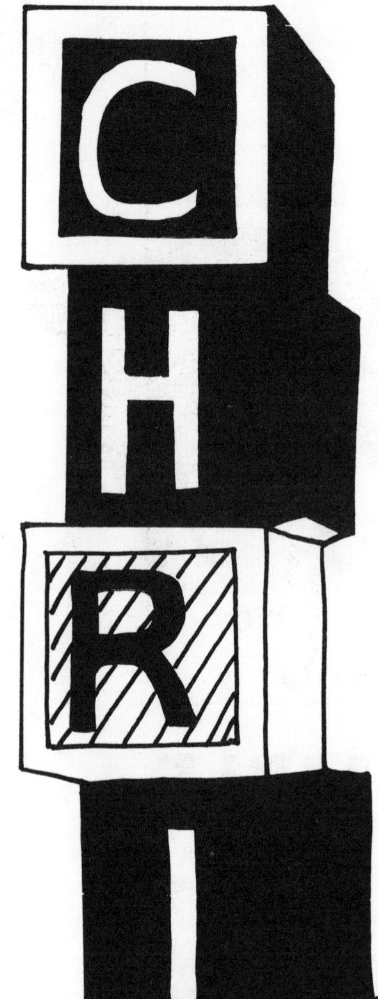

ACTIONS DO TELL!!

The Bible often reminds us that people who love God will live and behave in a way that will honor Him. For each letter in the word **Christian**, think of one characteristic of Christian living that will please God and show others that a person belongs to Him. Use your words to complete the acrostic.

C____________________

H____________________

R____________________

I____________________

S____________________

T____________________

I____________________

A____________________

N____________________

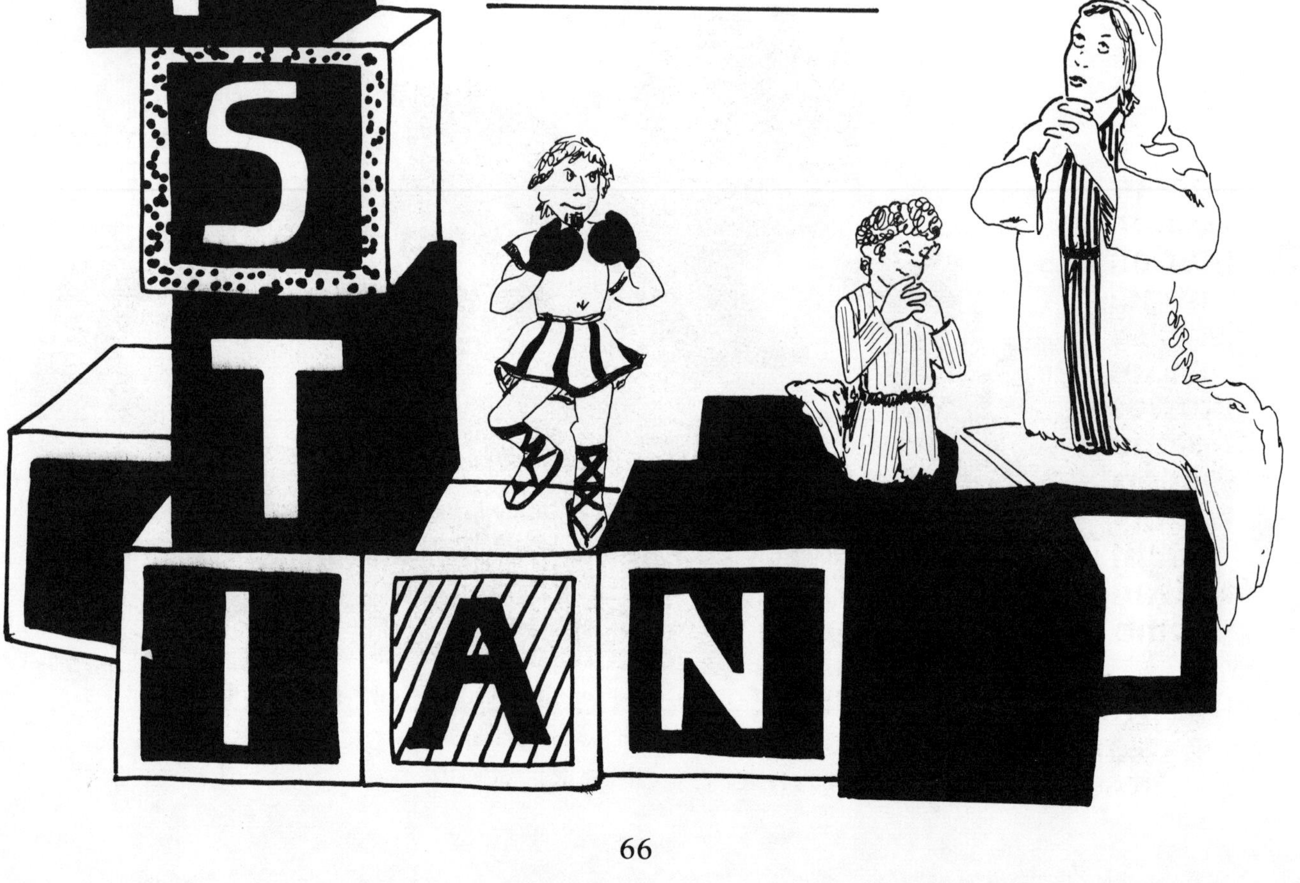

HE'S ALIVE!!

Write each word in its correct place on the acrostic. Then tell what each word has to do with the Resurrection story.

R
__ __ __ __ __ __ __ __

E
c r o s s e s

S
__ __ __ __ __ __

U
__ __ __ __ __ __ __

R
__ __ __ __ __

R
__ __ __ __ __ __

E
__ __ __ __ __ __ __ __

C
__ __ __ __ __ __

T
__ __ __ __ __

I
__ __ __ __ __ __ __

O

N
__ __ __ __ __ __ __ __

Joseph
garden
angel
disciples
thunder
crosses
stone
soldiers
Mary
Christ
forgiven
tomb

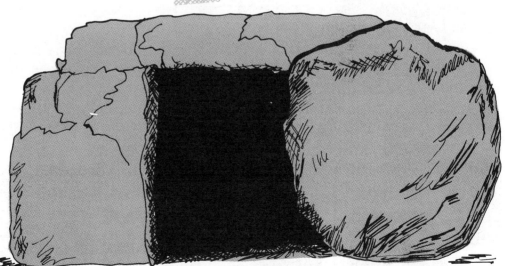

When you have finished, whisper a "Thank You!" to God for sending His Son, Jesus, to die for you. Then be glad that Jesus rose up from the grave to be alive for you!!

The Sun Stood Still...

Then It Moved Backward!

One day, Joshua was in the midst of an important battle with the Amorites. He was winning, but the sun was beginning to set, and he was afraid the enemy would escape in the darkness. So he prayed and asked God to stop the sun in the sky. God did just that! The sun stood still for almost 24 hours while Joshua won the battle. Impossible????? Not for God! (Joshua 10)

As if the Joshua story were not miraculous enough, God caused something even more strange and impossible to happen.

King Hezekiah's health was bad. The Lord had already told him that he needed to prepare himself to die, but the king was not ready to die. He was a good man and asked God to let him live 15 years longer. God sent the prophet Isaiah to tell Hezekiah the good news that He was going to answer his prayer with a big YES!

Well, Hezekiah could hardly believe it. He was skeptical. He asked for proof that God was really going to heal him and let him live. God said, "I will have the shadow on your sundial suddenly move forward 10 points or backward 10 points. Which way do you want it to move?" Hezekiah chose backward because he knew it would be more difficult or unusual for the sun to move backward ...... but that was no problem for God. Back the sun went, and the shadow on the sundial moved back with it. So the extra minutes that were left of the almost-24-hour day that the sun stood still for Joshua were used by this event in Hezekiah's life ...... and a whole extra day was added to time! (2 Kings 20)

Isn't God clever? He is the author of law and order, and He always knows how to make things come out just perfect!!

68

jumbled jabber

Read each jumbled sentence. Cross out one word that does not belong. Then rearrange the sentence to read correctly on the lines below.

1. Cut while Delilah wicked hair Samson's slept Baal had he.

   _____

2. Disobeys and into command king's lions is a of Daniel the thrown den window.

   _____

3. Love the thy all thou with God shalt thy commandment Lord heart.

   _____

4. Rebuilt in and Nehemiah wall 52 Jerusalem's days his Babylon friends.

   _____

5. Raised Jairus' from daughter the was dead servant.

   _____

6. Goliath won horns Gideon's jars battle army with and the.

   _____

7. Do you do you unto unto would them others have golden as.

   _____

8. Donkey angel times beat his Balaam three.

   _____

Fill in the correct answers, and the words will read the same across and down.

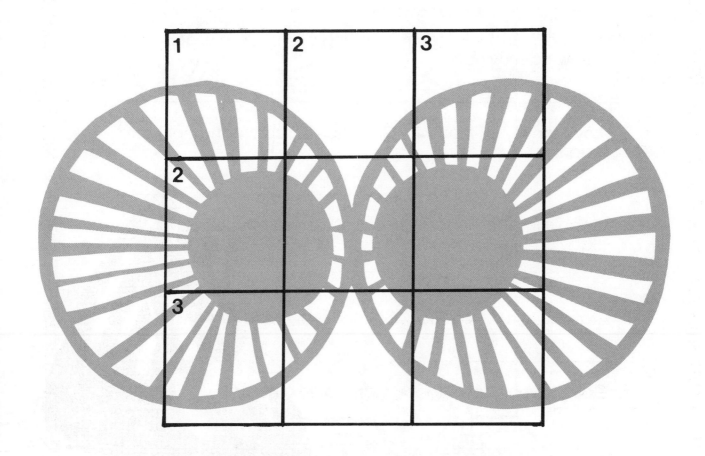

1. Jesus Christ is God's only _____
2. The number of true gods there are.
3. Used to catch fish.

me and my dad

Can you match the child in the left column with his father in the right column? Draw a line between them to show who belongs to whom.

A.   Isaac

B.   Zacharias

1.   Jonathan

C.   Jesse

2.   David

D.   Noah

3.   Benjamin

E.   Abraham

4.   Esau

F.   Saul

5.   Cain

G.   Ahasuerus

6.   John the Baptist

H.   Adam

7.   Ham

I.   David

8.   Isaac

J.   Jacob

9.   Darius

10. Solomon

FISHERMEN FOUR

Peter, James, John, and Andrew were fishing one night and got their lines all tangled. One of them caught a fish.
Put an **X** on the lucky fisherman.

A FAMILY TREE

The names of six famous ancestors of Joseph, the earthly father of Jesus, are listed without the first and the last letters. Can you complete the names using the letters hidden in the tree? Each letter can be used only once.

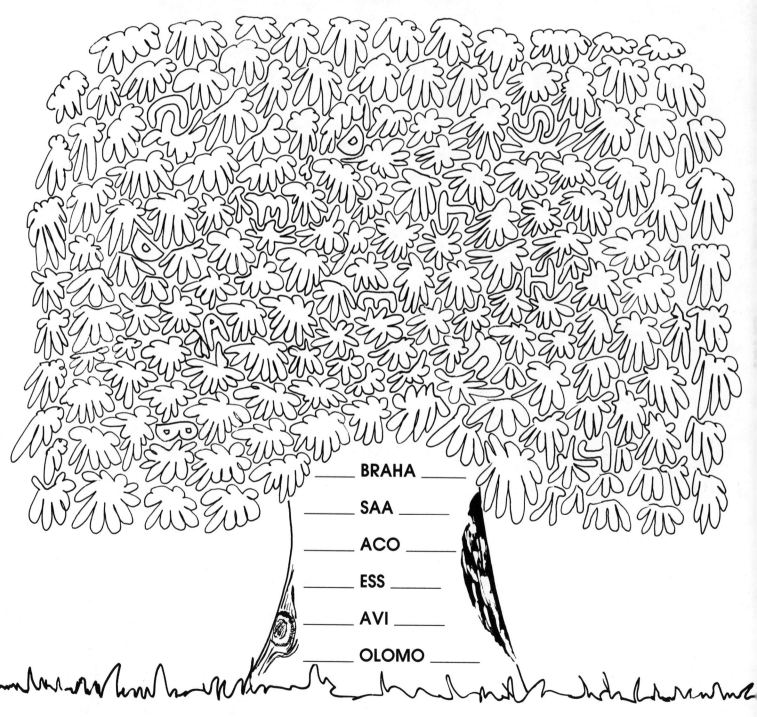

_____ BRAHA _____

_____ SAA _____

_____ ACO _____

_____ ESS _____

_____ AVI _____

_____ OLOMO _____

half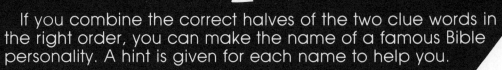

If you combine the correct halves of the two clue words in the right order, you can make the name of a famous Bible personality. A hint is given for each name to help you.

Ex. li**ma** **fur**y   **Mary** _____,
the mother of Jesus

1. sample season _____,
tricked by Delilah

2. racket helmet _____,
Jacob's beloved wife

3. market thatch _____,
sister to Lazarus and Mary

4. esteem herald _____,
a queen who saved her people

5. candor castle _____,
a woman always helping others

6. demand reward _____,
Peter's fisherman, disciple brother

7. jailer walrus _____,
whose daughter Jesus raised from the dead

8. rude thaw _____,
married Boaz and was David's great-grandmother

9. luck keep _____,
a physician and author of two books of the Bible

10. brad _____,
the first man

tram

half

JIGSAW JUMBLE

This jigsaw puzzle contains the name John the Baptist gave to Jesus. To find out what the name is, rewrite the letters in order by looking for the puzzle pieces that would fit together. The beginning and ending pieces have a straight side.

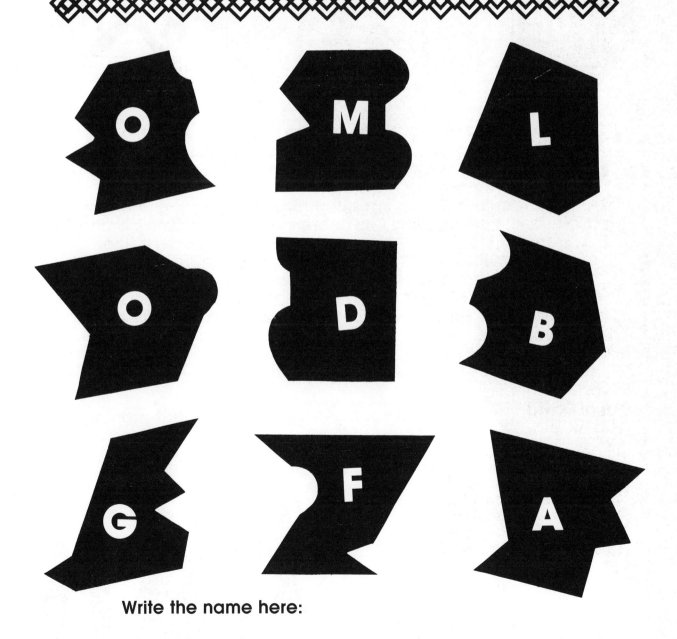

Write the name here:

___ ___ ___ ___ ___ ___ ___ ___

copy cat

If you go to school, you are probably already familiar with **symbols.** Perhaps you could read these symbols before you learned to read words. Can you identify them?

A symbol is anything that is used to represent something else. Often it is a picture. Symbols are sometimes better than words, because people of many different languages can understand them.

The Christian faith has symbols too. Some are older than the Bible itself. Here you find five Hebrew or Christian symbols and their meanings. Copy each one in the space beside it. Then cover the meanings, and see if you can remember what each symbol represents. You may find some of these symbols in your church. Sometimes several shapes are combined to create a new symbol. Next Sunday, look carefully for one or more of them.

Star of David

This represents Judaism and the modern country of Israel.

Star of David

76

Menorah

This seven-branch candlestick represents the Old Testament.

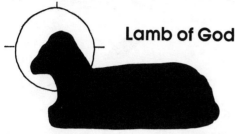

Lamb of God

This is a very common symbol for Christ. John the Baptist called him "the Lamb of God."

Dove

This is the most common symbol for the Holy Spirit (God's presence and power in people.)

Butterfly

This symbol is used to stand for "new life." We see it representing Easter, the celebration of Jesus' Resurrection.

Menorah

Lamb of God

Dove

Butterfly

NOAH'S SURPRISE

Break the code and find out how the rabbits plan to surprise Noah! Write your translation in the talk balloons below.

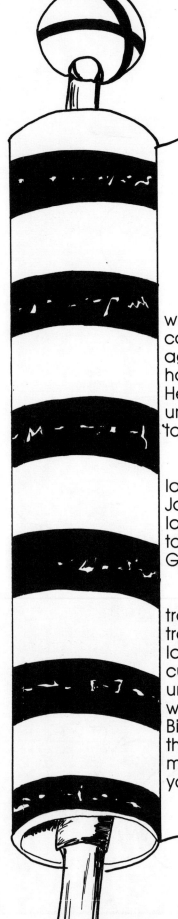

A Very Old Message Told Many New Ways

A long time ago, God gave His Word to some men who wrote down carefully what He told them. These writings were called manuscripts, and they were copied over and over again so that many people could read the message God had given. The first manuscripts were written in Greek and Hebrew since those were the languages the first writers understood. Later, when people of other languages wanted to read God's words, they had to be translated.

One of the most important translations into our English language was the King James translation (named for King James I). Translators who understood the Greek and Hebrew languages as well as the English worked very long and hard to make the English words say exactly the same message God had given to the first writers.

Since the King James translation, many other English translators have done the same thing. Each group has translated the words of the original manuscripts into the language that is normal for the people of their time and culture so that it would be easy for folks like you to read and understand. On the next page, you will see a Bible verse written as it appears in several different translations of the Bible. Read each translation carefully. Then choose the one that helps you understand God's words the very best and memorize it so that His ways will always be a part of the way you think and behave.

I Timothy 4:12

"Let no man despise thy youth; but be thou an example of the believers, in word, in conversation, in charity, in spirit, in faith, in purity."

— King James Version

"Don't let anyone think little of you because you are young. Be their ideal; let them follow the way you teach and live; be a pattern for them in your love, your faith, and your clean thoughts."

— The Living Bible

"Let no one despise your youth, but set the believers an example in speech and conduct, in love, in faith, in purity."

— Revised Standard Version

"Let no one slight you because you are young, but make yourself an example to believers in speech and behaviour, in love, fidelity, and purity."

— New English Bible

"Don't let anyone look down on you because you are young: see that they look up to you because you are an example to believers in your speech and behaviour, in your love and faith and sincerity."

— Phillips Modern English

"Do not let people disregard you because you are young, but be an example to all the believers in the way you speak and behave, and in your love, your faith and your purity."

— Jerusalem Bible

"Don't let anyone look down on you because you are young, but set an example for the believers in speech, in life, in love, in faith and in purity."

— New International Version

L O T S   O'   L U G G A G E

Play this game with a friend. Pretend you are going on a trip. You are going to take with you a whole Bible alphabet of objects, characters, and creatures. See if you can fill in the space on each suitcase with the name of a Bible object, character, or creature which begins with the correct letter. Take turns so that each of you will have to carry just half of the heavy luggage.

Circle what you believe will be your **heaviest** suitcase. Ask your friend to put an X on the suitcase that will be **easiest** for him or her to carry.

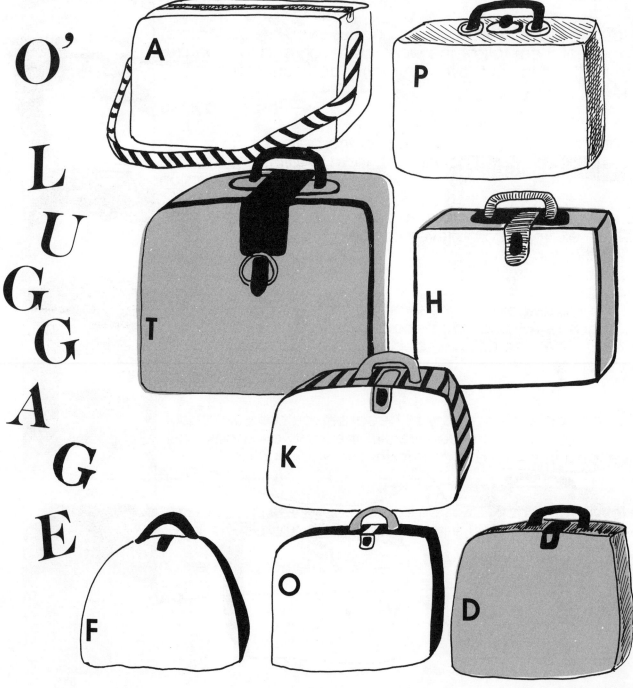

82

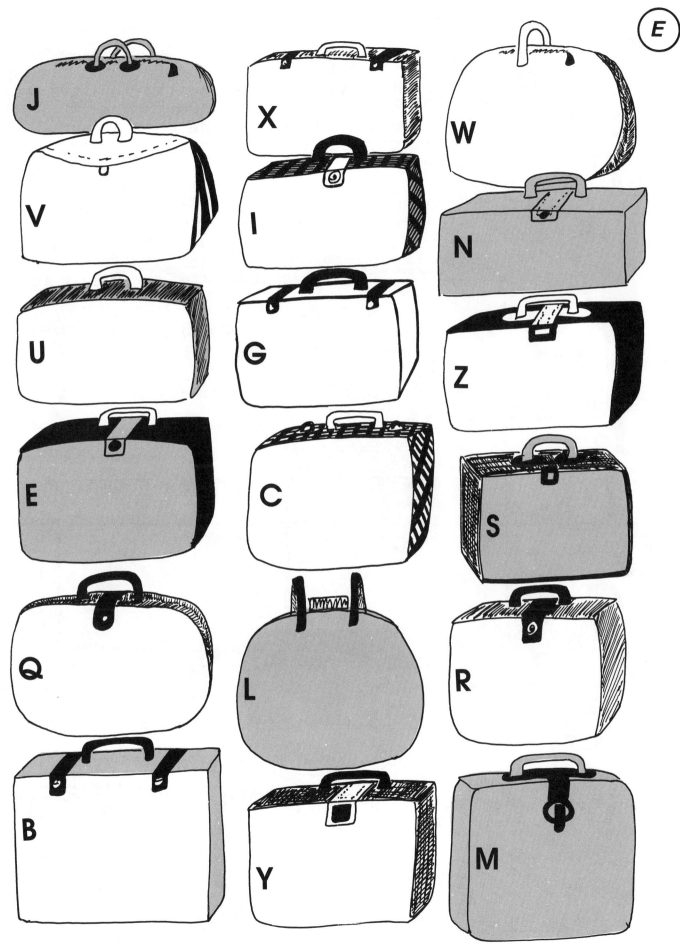

FINDERS, KEEPERS

Play this game by yourself or invite a friend to have a contest with you by doing the opposite page at the same time. (The first one to finish wins.)

Answer each question by looking up the verse in a King James Bible. Write your answers. Then draw a line from each answer to a matching picture hidden in the border on this page. You will discover that these two pages are equal but different.

You're going to need . . .

1. What was "thorny" in Mark 15:17?

2. Whom did Stephen look like in Acts 2:2?

3. What are we told to give our enemy to eat in Proverbs 25:21?

4. What large, hairy animal did King Solomon's navy bring to him in I Kings 10:22?

5. What provides light and is not hidden in Luke 8:16?

6. What is clean in Psalm 51:10?

7. What token of God's promise did Noah see after the flood in Genesis 9:16?

8. What has five attachments that can wiggle and is mentioned in Job 23:11?

9. What has one eye and is mentioned in Luke 18:25?

10. What came down on Jesus in Matthew 3:16?

A Scavenger Hunt For One or Two

Play this game by yourself or invite a friend to have a contest with you by doing the opposite page at the same time. (The first one to finish wins.)

Answer each question by looking up the verse in a King James Bible. Write your answers. Then draw a line from each answer to a matching picture hidden in the border on this page. You will discover that these two pages are equal but different.

. . . a King James Bible for this one!

1. What was eaten with bread in Mark 6:41?

2. What was broken in Acts 2:42?

3. What is like a good medicine in Proverbs 17:22?

4. To what does God compare the Pharaoh of Egypt in Ezekiel 29:3?

5. If you have two of these, Luke 3:11 says to give one away. What is it?

6. What is planted by the rivers of water in Psalm 1:3?

7. What was found in Benjamin's sack in Genesis 44:12?

8. What has five attachments that can wiggle and is mentioned in Job 40:14?

9. What does Jesus tell us to "take up daily" in Luke 9:23?

10. What was seen in the east in Matthew 2:2?

...PATH..TO..

This is the story of a man who was told to go the River Jordan to be cured of a disease. To complete the sentences in his story, follow his path to the river. Start with **N**, and write down **every other letter**.

Return from the river coming up the same path. Start with **E** at the river, and write down **every other letter** as you continue to fill in the blanks in the story.

To get you started on the right path, the first word in the story is completed for you.

Start:

N L A A A E M R A S N T L F E

B I E R Y A S M K A I S N L H

A O E D L E I S S U H F A E S

86

...A..BATH...

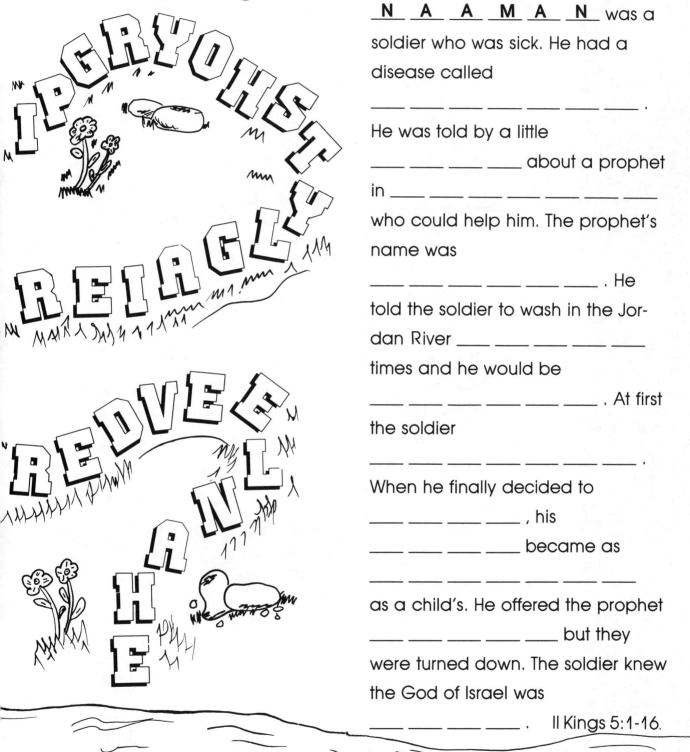

__N__ __A__ __A__ __M__ __A__ __N__ was a soldier who was sick. He had a disease called

___ ___ ___ ___ ___ ___ ___ ___ .

He was told by a little

___ ___ ___ ___ about a prophet

in ___ ___ ___ ___ ___ ___ ___

who could help him. The prophet's name was

___ ___ ___ ___ ___ ___ ___ . He told the soldier to wash in the Jordan River ___ ___ ___ ___

times and he would be

___ ___ ___ ___ ___ ___ . At first the soldier

___ ___ ___ ___ ___ ___ ___ ___ .

When he finally decided to

___ ___ ___ ___ , his

___ ___ ___ ___ became as

___ ___ ___ ___ ___ ___ ___

as a child's. He offered the prophet

___ ___ ___ ___ ___ but they were turned down. The soldier knew the God of Israel was

___ ___ ___ ___ ___ . II Kings 5:1-16.

Each name of a Bible personality has the name of one of the pictured items hidden in it. Underline the hidden word in the name and draw a line to its picture.

Adam

Abraham

Jacob

Bathsheba

Herod

Hosea

Martha

Samson

James

Mark

WHAT'S IN A NAME?

Naaman
Timothy
Philemon
Matthew
Abednego
Stephen
Cornelius
Caleb
Delilah
Barnabas

JOE'S DELI

WELCOME

GINGER

Each name of a Bible personality has the name of one of the pictured items hidden in it. Underline the hidden word in the name and draw a line to its picture.

STRAIGHT A's AAAAAAAAAA

Read the clues on the opposite page. Then try to fill in the correct names of each Bible place or character. Use the Bible references to check your answers and enjoy some very exciting stories.

A __ __ __ __ __ A

A __ A __

A __ __ __ __ __ __ __ __

A __ __ __ __ A __ __

A __ A __

A __ __ __ A __

A __ __ __ __ __ A

A __ __ __

A __ __ A __ __ __ __

A __ __ A

A __ A __ A __

A __ __ A __ A __

A __ A __ __ A __

A __ __ __ __ __ __

A __ __ __ A __ __ A

A king who pardoned Paul
from prison.
Acts 25:13 - 26:32

A tentmaker of Corinth
and a friend of Paul.
Acts 18:1-3

Another word for father.
Mark 14:36

The town of Joseph, the man
who convinced Pilate to let
him bury Jesus' body in his
own new tomb.
Matthew 27:57-60

A son of King David, caught
by his hair in a tree while
riding a donkey.
II Samuel 18:9

Husband of Jezebel, a
worshiper of Baal, who had
a contest with Elijah to see
whose God could send fire
and rain.
I Kings 18:17-46

The mountain on which
Noah's ark rested.
Genesis 8:4

Brother of Simon Peter.
Matthew 4:18

A Hebrew boy, saved from
the fiery furnace.
Daniel 1:7

A shepherd son of Adam.
Genesis 4:2

Wife of Nabal, and later,
of King David.
II Samuel 3:3

He stole some treasures after
the fall of Jericho & was
stoned for his deed.
Joshua 7:1

Lost a rib to a woman.
Genesis 2:22

He and his wife kept money
they had promised to God
and lied about it.
Acts 5:1-5

A man of great faith, and a
friend of God.
James 2:23

Rebus Riddles

1 B + 👁 + 🐂 = ☐ ☐ ☐ ☐ ☐

2 J + 🌽 = ☐ ☐ ☐ ☐ ☐

3 🤐 = ☐ ☐ ☐ ☐

4 🥧 + ♪ do re mi fa sol la ti do + t = ☐ ☐ ☐ ☐ ☐ ☐

5 S + 🍲 = ☐ ☐ ☐ ☐ ☐ ☐

Look carefully at each rebus picture and try to "sound out" the Bible word it suggests. Write the correct answer by each picture.

92

6

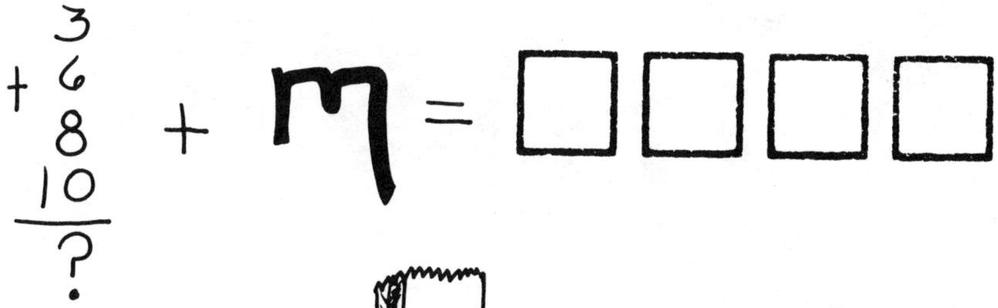

$$\begin{array}{r} 3 \\ 6 \\ 8 \\ + \ 10 \\ \hline ? \end{array}$$

+ ⴘ = ☐ ☐ ☐ ☐

7 👁 + 🛍 = ☐ ☐ ☐ ☐ ☐

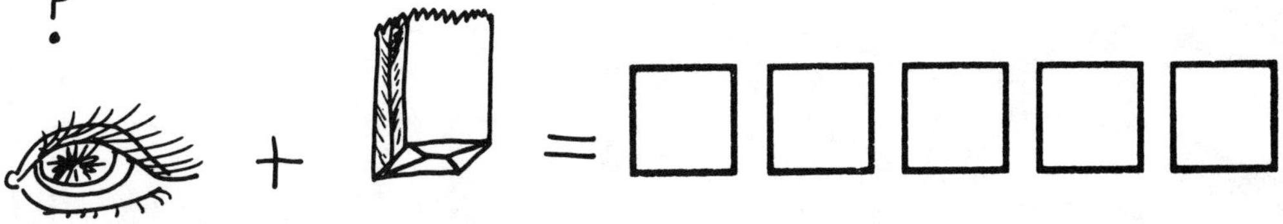

8 + = ☐ ☐ ☐ ☐ ☐

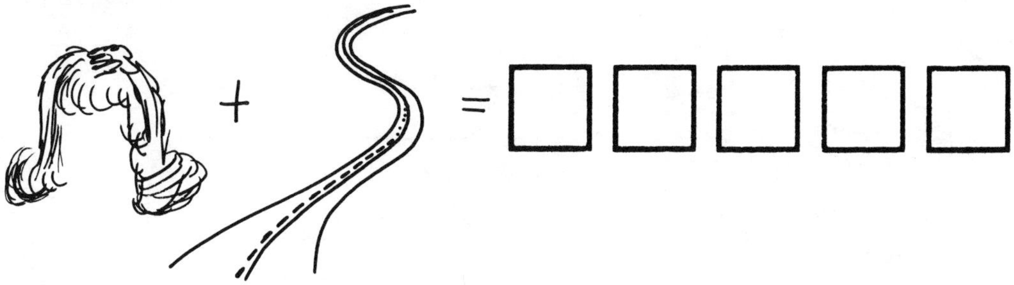

9 E + = ☐ ☐ ☐ ☐ ☐

10  + WHOO! WHOO! = ☐ ☐ ☐ ☐

11 e + = ☐ ☐ ☐

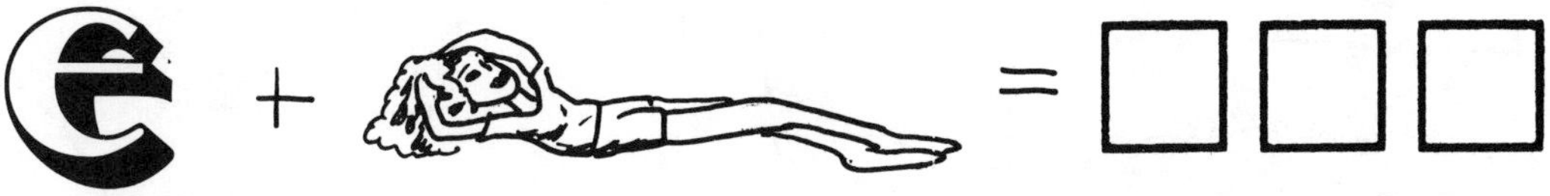

12 + = ☐ ☐ ☐ ☐ ☐ ☐ ☐

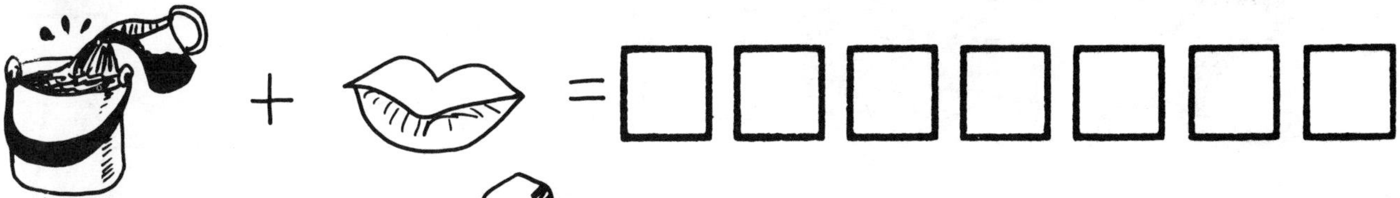

13 + = ☐ ☐ ☐ ☐ ☐

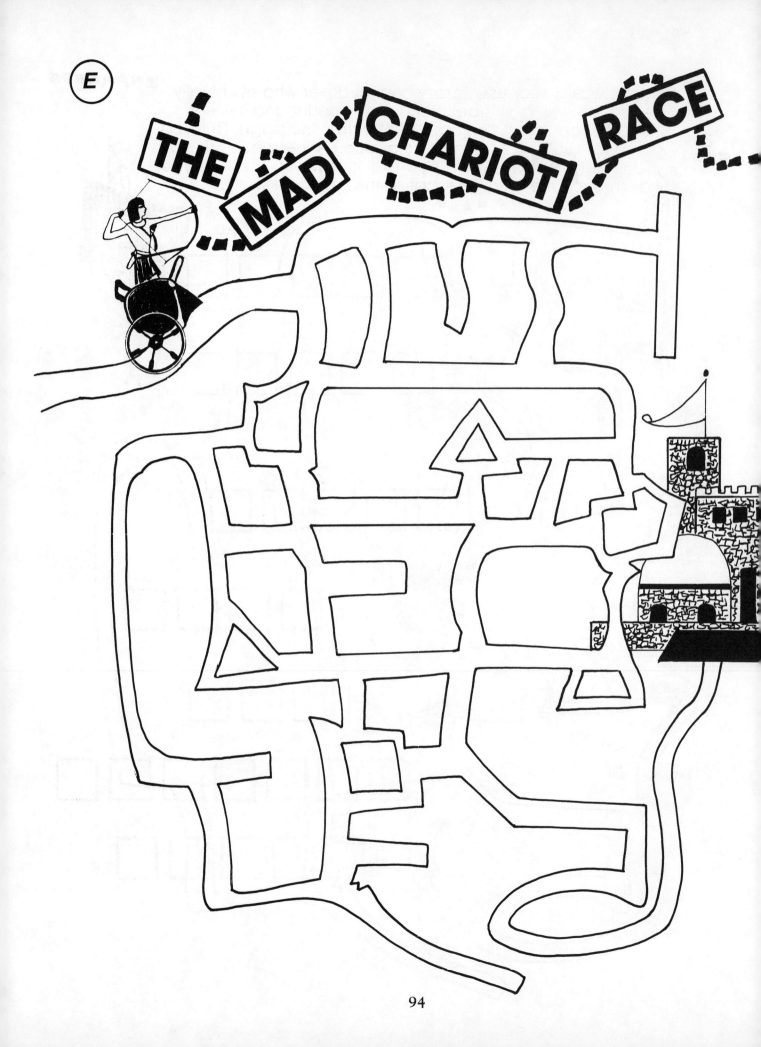

94

Jehu was a reckless, crazy chariot driver who eventually became the king of Israel. Hop on his chariot and invite a friend to hop on with his opponent across the page. (This is a game for two . . . . and it's a race!) Ask someone to start you off with a loud "GO." See which one of you can ride your way through the tangled roads to the palace first.

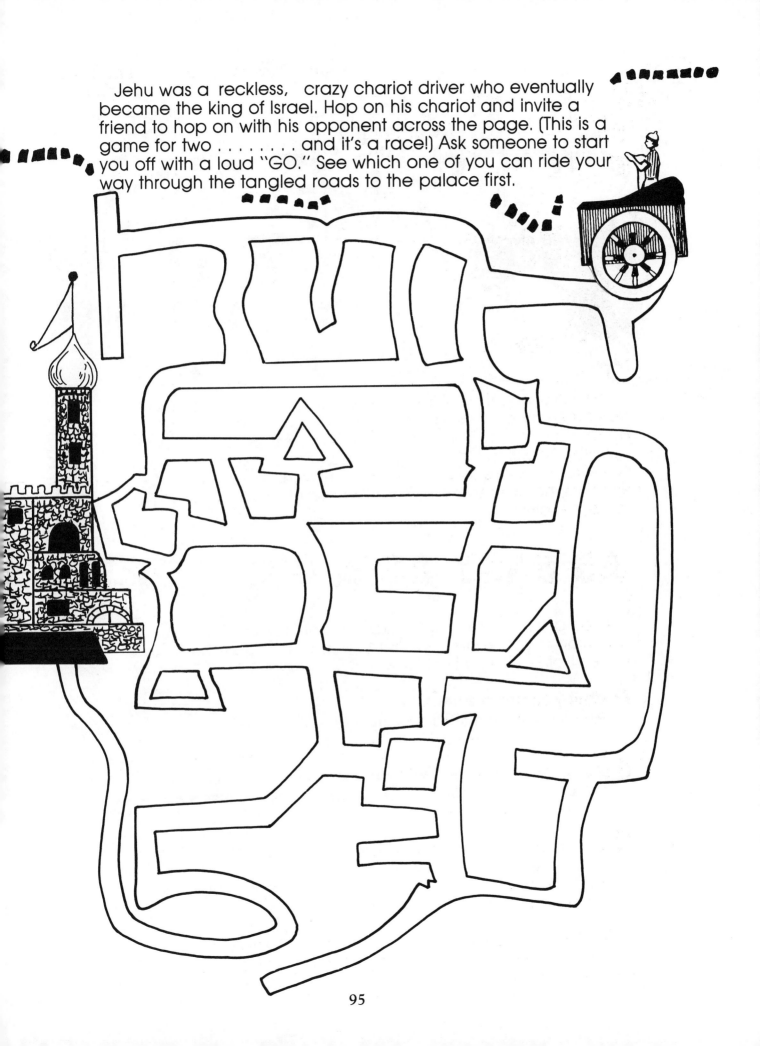

The Bible says that all people are sinners. But Jesus died to pay for every bad thing we have ever said or thought or done. He says that if we believe in Him and ask Him to forgive our sins, He will make a home in heaven for us and take us to live with Him there forever. God cannot lie. So He will do for us exactly what He promises. How wonderful! Think about it! Tell someone else!

AS EASY AS A B C ....

If you are not sure how to explain God's wonderful plan for salvation to someone else, get to know the simple facts and verses below. They will help you.

A dmit you are a sinner.
"All have sinned and come short of the glory of God."
(Romans 3:23)

B elieve Jesus can and will save you from your sins.
"Believe on the Lord Jesus Christ, and thou shalt be saved ..."
(Acts 16:31)

C onfess to God your sin. Talk to Him aloud. Tell Him that you believe He has died to forgive your sin. Let Him know that you want Him to be the most important thing in your life from now on.

"If thou shalt Confess with thy mouth the Lord Jesus and shalt believe in thine heart that God hath raised him from the dead, thou shalt be saved." *(Romans 10:9)*

96

Study the A B C plan for sharing the Good News of God's forgiveness and salvation.
Try to memorize it along with the Bible verses.

On this page, see if you can rewrite from memory each part of the A B C plan and give the Bible reference for each part.
(Practice looking up each verse in your Bible so that you can find them easily if you should want to share them with a friend.)

A

_____

_____

_____

                                    _____

B

_____

_____

_____

                                    _____

C

_____

_____

_____

_____

_____

                                    _____

Name That Book! ...

Each book title should remind you of one of these books of the Bible: **Acts, Daniel, Esther, Exodus, Genesis, Job, Jonah, Joshua, Proverbs, Psalms, Revelation or Ruth.**

Complete the crossword puzzle on the opposite page with the appropriate names of books of the Bible.

HOW TO SURVIVE A FLOOD

3 - Down

A MOST PATIENT MAN

4 - Across

HOW TO CATCH LARGE FISH

4 - Down

THE WALLS CAME TUMBLING DOWN

10 - Across

A LOOK AT THINGS TO COME

2 - Across

GOOD ADVICE FOR DAILY LIVING

1 - Down

KING DAVID'S GREAT-GRANNY

11 - Across

HOLY MOSES!

9 - Down

A QUEEN SAVES HER PEOPLE

8 - Across

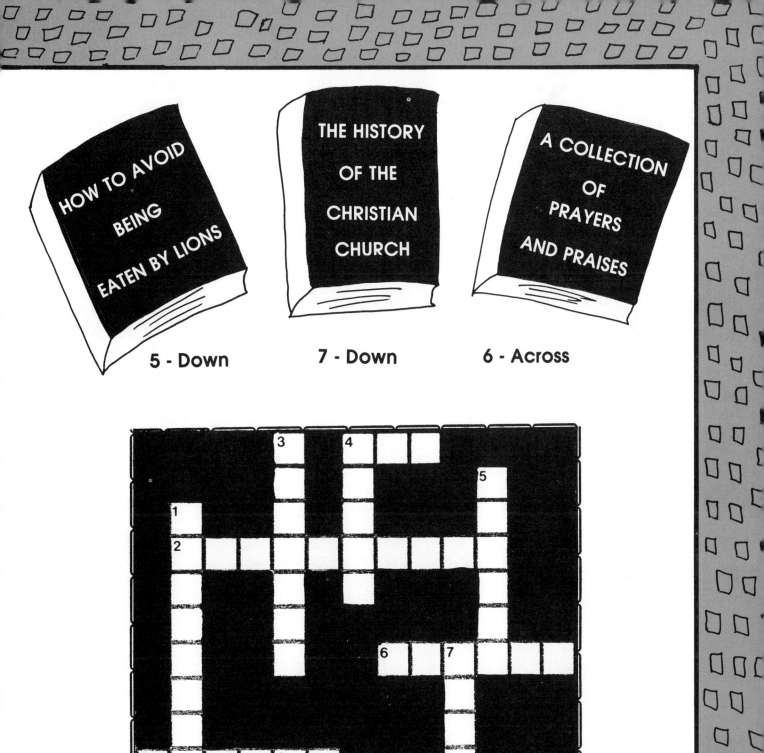

HOW TO AVOID BEING EATEN BY LIONS

5 - Down

THE HISTORY OF THE CHRISTIAN CHURCH

7 - Down

A COLLECTION OF PRAYERS AND PRAISES

6 - Across

DO YOU COMPUTE?

If you can answer all the questions below with the correct number and add and subtract correctly as you go, you will finish up with the number found in the verse, Revelation 1:12. Try it!

How many times did Simon Peter deny Jesus?
(Luke 22:61) _____

How many books are in the New Testament?
(Matthew - Revelation) + _____

How many sons did Jacob have?
(Gen. 42:13) - _____

For how many pieces of silver did Joseph's brothers sell him?   (Genesis 37:28) + _____

How many commandments did God give us through Moses? (Exodus 34:28) - _____

How old was Jesus when Joseph and Mary found Him teaching in the temple? (Luke 2:42) - _____

How many disciples did Jesus have?(Matthew 10:1) - _____

How many sons did Noah have? (Genesis 6:10) + _____

Total _____

REBUS ARITHMETIC

What town was King David's childhood home?

What king pretended he was a madman to escape his enemies?

Rewrite each puzzle using words in place of the pictures. After adding and subtracting all the letters in each puzzle, you will have just the right letters to form the answer to the question at the top of each puzzle. You will have to rearrange the letters.

THE FRAME - UP

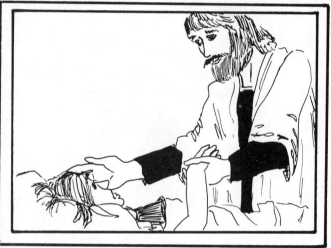

Color the frames around the pictures that show something Jesus did.

what a name!!

Jesus
Nazarene
Everlasting Father
Prince of Peace
Truth
Wonderful
Alpha
Messiah
Lily of the Valley
Light
Lamb
Rose of Sharon
Morning Star
Good Shepherd
Omega
Emmanuel
Rabbi
Son of God
Son of Man
Christ
Mighty God
Word
The Way
Door
Life
Master
Savior
Counselor

In the Bible, Jesus is called by many different names. All of them are very special. Find these special names in the puzzle and circle them.

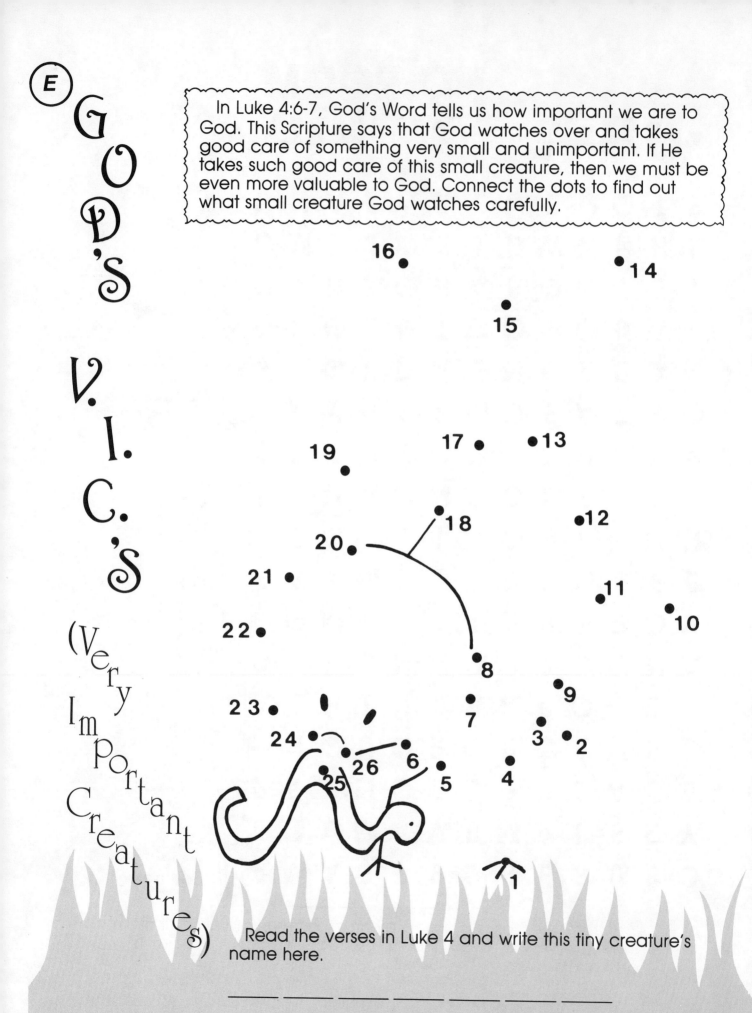

(E) GOD'S V.I.C.'S (Very Important Creatures)

In Luke 4:6-7, God's Word tells us how important we are to God. This Scripture says that God watches over and takes good care of something very small and unimportant. If He takes such good care of this small creature, then we must be even more valuable to God. Connect the dots to find out what small creature God watches carefully.

16   14
15
17   13
19
18
20   12
21
11
22   10
8
23   9
7
24   3   2
26   6
25   5   4
1

Read the verses in Luke 4 and write this tiny creature's name here.

_____ _____ _____ _____ _____ _____ _____

NO ROOM

Mary and Joseph have just arrived in Bethlehem. They are tired, and Mary is going to have a baby. They have been told there are no rooms at any of the inns. Help them find some place to stay.

A SPECIAL SECRET

1	2	3	4	5	6

In the Bible, there is a story about a very strong man who was tricked by a woman named Delilah. He told her a very special secret about himself. His secret was that his long hair made him strong. One night while he slept, she sneaked in and had his hair cut. He was weak, so his enemies captured him, and he became a slave. Later, when his hair grew long, he became strong once more and was able to push down the whole temple. Find his name by placing the first letter of each object pictured in its numbered square.

A MYSTERY MEAL

In this picture, Jesus is preaching to thousands of people. Soon they will be hungry, and Jesus will turn two fish and five loaves of bread into enough food for all the crowd. Find the two fish and the five loaves of bread hidden in this picture.

CODED COMMANDMENTS

The Pharisees wanted to trick Jesus into speaking against the Law so they asked Him to name the greatest commandment. Jesus gave them an answer in which they could find no fault. You will discover what He said if you can break the coded message below.

First clue: The first two words are **LOVE** and **THE** and **Z** stands for **A**.

KNUD SGD KNQC XNTQ FNC VHSG ZKK XNTQ GDZQS,

RNTK, ZMC LHMC. SGD RDBNMC HR, KNUD XNTQ MDH FGANQ

ZR LTBG ZR XNT KNUD XNTQRDKE. JDDO NMKX SGDRD ZMC

XNT VHKK EHMC SGZS XNT ZQD NADXHMF ZKK SGD NSGDQR.

(Paraphrased from Matthew 22:27-40 TLB)

Second clue: Read this only if you are having trouble: Each letter in the code represents the one following it in the alphabet.

Write the decoded message here:

_____

_____

_____

_____

THREE by THREE

In each of the nine squares in this "3 x 3," describe a Bible story which pairs up the category at the top with each of the numbers on the left side. For example, the square in the middle will require a description of a story which involves **2 women.**

	Men	**Women**	**Angels**
1			
2			
3 (or more)			

If you can't think of a story for one of the squares, use the Scripture reference here to find one. Read the story, and then describe it in your own words.

	Men	**Women**	**Angels**
1	John 9:1-34	John 4:4-42	Luke 1:26-38
2	Luke 24:13-35	I Kings 3:16-28	Genesis 19:1-16
3 (or more)	Matthew 26:17-30	Exodus 2:1-10	Genesis 28:10-22

These sentences are all mixed up. See if you can set them straight by rearranging the words and writing each one correctly.

1. Loves you God much very.

_____

2. From light Saul blinded heaven a.

_____

3. Jail from angel escape Peter helped an.

_____

4. Gave a poor food Elijah widow.

_____

5. Dead from Lazarus raised was the.

_____

6. Thirty Judas of Jesus silver betrayed for pieces.

_____

110

GOOD NEWS! (E)

Use the first letter of each object to write the GOOD NEWS message below!

SOUND-ALIKES

Each word in this list is a rhyming word for a Bible name. Use the space beside each word to fill in a Bible name that has the same ending sound.

madam _____Adam_____

tall_____

sweeter _____

on _____

Clara _____

pot _____

noses _____

even_____

Karen _____

boa _____

hairy_____

park_____

duke _____

globe _____

names_____

bouquet_____

manual _____

jail_____

banana _____

famous _____

plane _____

Mona _____

leave _____

yam _____

112

For Thinkers Only ...

ODD MAN OUT

Decide which word or phrase does NOT belong in each group. Cross it out. Then use the space at the end of each line to tell WHY it does not belong.

1. John Job Luke James Titus _____

2. Peter Paul James Andrew Thomas _____

3. Reuben Moses Joseph Levi Benjamin _____
   _____

4. Jerusalem Philadelphia Sodom Los Angeles Nineveh
   _____

5. Elijah Micah Peter Jeremiah Isaiah _____

6. Queen of Sheba Esther Delilah Jezebel Vashti _____
   _____

7. Hannah Eve Rebekah Moriah Elisabeth _____
   _____

8. Adam Ahab Joash Herod Solomon _____
   _____

9. Boils Hail Locusts Frogs Snakes _____

10. Water Fire Wind Ring Dove _____

11. Two fish Bottle of perfume Manna from heaven
    Cruse of oil Jugs of water _____

12. Matthew Ruth Isaiah Jonah Ezra _____

A KIND CROSSWORD PUZZLE

This puzzle is filled with words that give you that "warm, fuzzy" feeling. These words are found often in the Bible. Here, they are spelled in an unusual way. Figure out what is wrong with the spelling, and write the words correctly. Then fill them in this very "kind-word" puzzle.

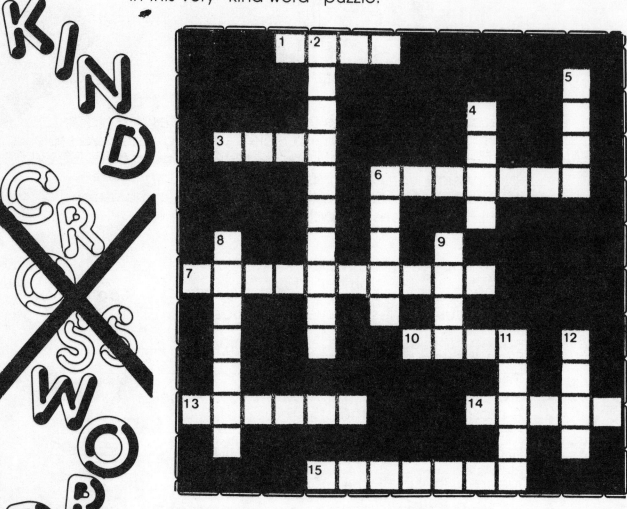

Down:
2. dnatsrednu _____
4. doog _____
5. dnik _____
6. sselb _____
8. trofmoc _____
9. evol _____
11. ecaep _____
12. epoh _____

Across:
1. tsuj _____
3. erac _____
6. devoleb _____
7. noissapmoc _____
10. pleh _____
13. dneirf _____
14. yppah _____
15. evigrof _____

114

HIDE & SEEK

In these sentences, names of Bible personalities are hidden. The spelling does not match the Bible's, so it might help you to read the sentences out loud as you "seek" each name.

	Answer
Ex: Do you **know a** good recipe for fudge?	**Noah**
The beavers build **a dam** in our creek.	**Adam**

1. Even though she was the smallest girl on the team, she batted in a run. _____

2. A mosquito just bit me! _____

3. With the help of a cane, Grandpa is able to walk. _____ and _____

4. I have a lot of homework. _____

5. If you don't study math, you won't know how to balance your checkbook when you grow up. _____

6. It's appalling how many people are sick with the flu. _____

7. After three months of flying lessons, I get to solo Monday. _____

8. Mark my word, it will snow soon. _____

9. I like my bath lukewarm. _____

10. Catholics go to Mass. _____

MASKED MESSAGE

This is a letter that might have been written from one early Christian family to another during a time when Christians were persecuted for their faith. It appears to be a friendly letter, but is actually a <u>code</u> letter that contains a secret message or request. Read the letter carefully. The special "code" words are underlined to help you figure out the secret message. Write the code words in order on the lines below and read the message aloud to yourself. What did Josh and Rachel want to tell Joel and Aquila?

Dear Joel and Aquila,

We are hoping to visit you on the next Sabbath day, but the <u>wheel</u> on our oxcart is broken and will not be repaired in time.

John and Andrea had dinner with us last week. They brought a delicious <u>meat</u> dish that was <u>fried,</u> and we all enjoyed it very much.

The boys have been raking <u>hay</u> for <u>two</u> weeks now. The <u>pea</u> crop is nearly ready for harvest. We <u>are</u> all working very hard toward <u>a</u> week of rest and relaxation. <u>Why</u> don't the <u>four</u> of you plan to join us?

Our old hound dog, Elijah, has hurt his <u>paw.</u> <u>All</u> he does is howl day and night, and we fear we may have to take him to Dr. Saul again.

We'll be looking forward to seeing you soon.

Sincerely,

Josh and Rachel

_____

_____

IF YOU'RE HAPPY, SHOUT

Each sentence tells about a letter that fits in one of the above spaces. Write the correct letter in the box above its number. Then you will know exactly what to do!!

5.	I'm **first** in	and **second** in
3.	I'm **last** in	and **first** in **LAST.**
1.	I'm **first** in	and **last** in
7.	I'm snug in the **middle** of **BUG** 'n **RUG.**	
9.	I'm the **beginning** and **end** of the **49th** U.S.. State.	
8.	I'm found **twice** in **JACOB'S PAJAMAS, never** in **ADAM'S APPLES.**	
2.	I'm **first** in	and **last** in
4.	I'm **twice** in	and **once** in
6.	I'm **single** in	and **double** in
10.	I'm **first** in	and	too!

117

In Mark 10:25, it is easier for me to get through the eye of a needle that for a rich man to get into heaven.

In Genesis 24:46, Rebekah gave me a drink from a well, and then Abraham's servant knew she was God's choice for Isaac's wife.

Color the picture to find out what I am.

COLOR CAPER

1 — Yellow   2 — Green   3 — Blue   4 — Red   5 — Brown

SOLOS, DUETS, & TRIOS

Use the clues to help you fill in the names of these famous Bible "musicians."

solos

D _ _ _ _ _ _ (Alone he fought a giant.)

D _ _ _ _ _ _ (Alone he stopped his master, Balaam.)

D _ _ _ _ _ (Alone he prayed 3 times a day . . . . and ended up in a den of lions!)

R _ _ _ _ _ (She protected the spies sent from Israel to Jericho.)

M _ _ _ (At first, she was the only one to know her Son would be the Savior.)

duets

R _ _ _ _ _ & N _ _ _ _ _
(best friends & in-laws!)

J _ _ _ _ _ & E _ _ _ _
(twin brothers)

A _ _ _ _ & E _ _
(the first duo ever)

M _ _ _ _ _ & A _ _ _ _ _
(Together they led the children of Israel in the wilderness.)

J _ _ _ _ _ _ & C _ _ _ _
(Together they were a good spy team!)

trios

S _ _ _ _ _ _ _ _ _ _ , A _ _ _ _ _ _ _ _
& M _ _ _ _ _ _ _ _ (A trio of friends in a fire!)

(The three who make up the Godhead)

F _ _ _ _ _ _ , S _ _
H _ _ _ S _ _ _ _

119

STEPS TO SUCCESS

To be afraid:

Ears do it:

Sits on your shoulders:

Not alive:

Do it to books:

Not fake:

A sea animal with flippers: **seal**

Read the word in bold print on the bottom step. Then change one letter of that word to get to the next step. Climb all the way up by changing only one letter on each step. The word at the top should complete this verse:

"The _____ of the Lord is the beginning of knowledge."
(Proverbs 1:7)

120

PICTURE

PERFECT (vertical)

At first glance, everything looks the same in these two pictures. However, there are ten differences. Circle the things that are different in the bottom picture.

At first glance, everything looks the same in these two pictures. However, there are ten differences. Circle the things that are different in the bottom picture.

PERFECT (vertical)

PICTURE

ONE ROYAL MESS!

1 _____

2 _____

3 _____

4 _____

5 _____

6 _____

7 _____

AHAB
BATHSHEBA
DAVID
ESTHER
JEZEBEL
SAUL
SOLOMON

Each figure represents a king or queen named in the Bible. On each one, the letters of his or her name are hidden. Find the letters and unscramble them to name each "royal" person.

122

$FUNNY MONEY$

In early Bible times, bartering was the most common form of trade. That means people just traded goods for other goods. However, because of the inconvenience of this, metals such as gold, silver, copper, and iron were made into coins. The "money" words listed here are from Bible times. Some of them are coins and some of them are units of weight. Find these words in the word-find puzzle.

PENNY
PIM
POUND
SHEKEL
TALENT
TETRADRACHM

BEKAH
DENARIUS
DRACHMA
FARTHING
MINAH
MITE

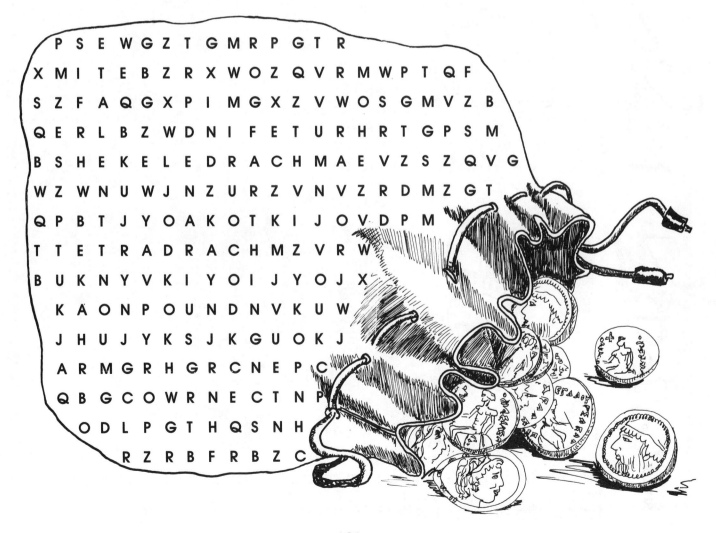

```
P S E W G Z T G M R P G T R
X M I T E B Z R X W O Z Q V R M W P T Q F
S Z F A Q G X P I M G X Z V W O S G M V Z B
Q E R L B Z W D N I F E T U R H R T G P S M
B S H E K E L E D R A C H M A E V Z S Z Q V G
W Z W N U W J N Z U R Z V N V Z R D M Z G T
Q P B T J Y O A K O T K I J O V D P M
T T E T R A D R A C H M Z V R W
B U K N Y V K I Y O I J Y O J X
K A O N P O U N D N V K U W
J H U J Y K S J K G U O K J
A R M G R H G R C N E P C
Q B G C O W R N E C T N P
O D L P G T H Q S N H
R Z R B F R B Z C
```

123

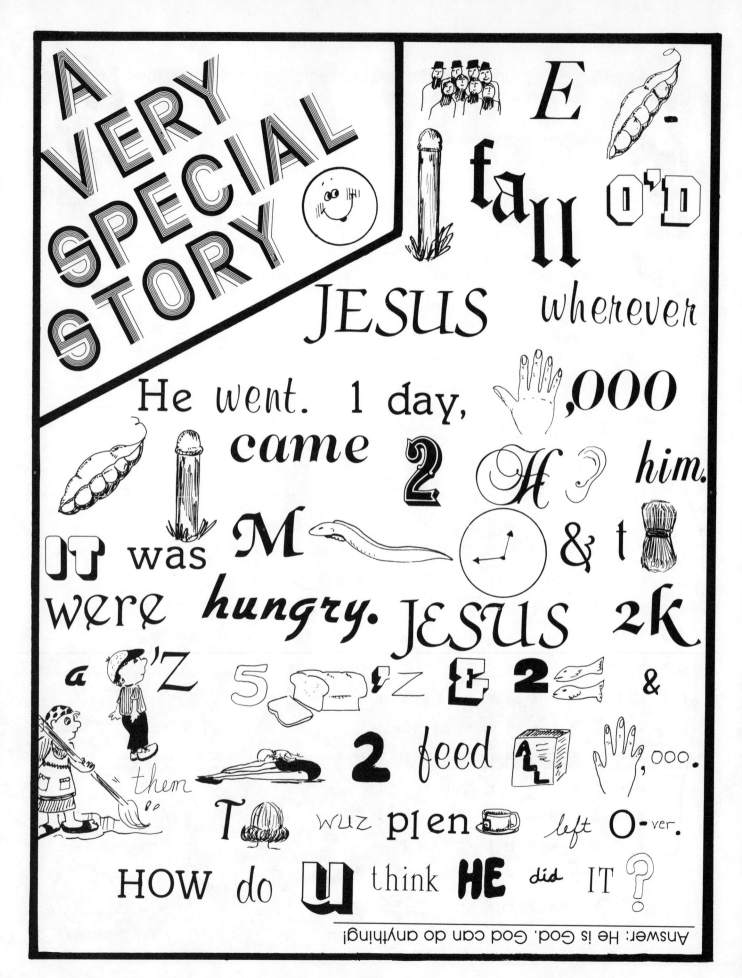

A VERY SPECIAL STORY

E

fall

O'D

JESUS

wherever

He went. 1 day, ,000 came 2 H? him.

IT was M ? & t

were hungry. JESUS 2K

a 'z 5 'z 2 &

2 feed ,000.

T wuz plen left O-ver.

HOW do U think **HE** did IT?

To read this important message, match the objects in the talk balloon with the key below.

Write the message here:

_____

_____

_____

_____ 2:5

2:5

	there		Christ			one
	and		is			Jesus
	man		between			God
	mediator		the			for
	First		men			Timothy

PICTURE CROSSWORD

E

Fill in the correct word to the right or below each picture. (The words are written below to help you with spelling, but they are **not** in the right order.) After you have finished the puzzle, see if you can tell a Bible story for each word.

jug, sun, tent, angel, lion, sling, coat, fish, candle, tree, bread, star, heart

EYES IN DISGUISE

In Proverbs 30, I am on a rock.
In Amos 9, I am in the bottom of the sea.
In Numbers 21, I am on a pole.
In Genesis 3, I am in a garden.
What am I?

Adam & Eve
The Garden
EARTH

Write my name here:

_____

Draw my picture here.

WORDS TO THE WISE

The Bible is full of good advice. Ephesians 4:26 is one verse that will help you get along with your friends and family. Find the following words, letter by letter. Then write them in the verse to discover a very important message that will help you in your daily living.

My first letter is in **sit** but not in **hit**,
My second letter is in **cup** and in **hut**,
My third letter is in **in** but not in **it**.   _____ _____ _____

My first letter is in **do** but not in **to**,
My second and third letters are in **low** and also in **row**,
My fourth letter is in **knit** but not in **kit**.

_____ _____ _____ _____

My first letter is in **hay** but not in **hey**,
My second and third letters are in **sling** and also in **fang**,
My fourth letter is in **her** and in **sir**,
My fifth letter is in **my** but not in **me**.

_____ _____ _____ _____ _____

"Don't let the ___ ___ ___ go ___ ___ ___ ___ with you still

___ ___ ___ ___ ___ ."   **(Ephesians 4:26 TLB)**

ALL FIRED UP!

Fire is mentioned many times in the Bible. It is one way God spoke to man; it is used to describe God's Word; it is a means of judgment; and it is to be the final and everlasting punishment.

Answer the following "fiery" questions with these names:
Moses, Elijah, Sodom, Gomorrah, Samson, Jesus, Israelites.

1 To whom did God appear in the form of a flaming bush?
(Exodus 3:2)

_____

2 Who set fire to the tails of foxes and sent them into the cornfields of the Philistines?
(Judges 15:4)

_____

3 What two evil cities were destroyed by brimstone and fire from heaven?
(Genesis 19:24)

_____

4 Who went to heaven in a chariot of fire driven by horses of fire?
(II Kings 2:11)

_____

5 Who will appear from heaven with angels in flaming fire to bring judgment to those who have not obeyed God's Word?
(II Thessalonians 1:7)

_____

6 Who was led through the Red Sea wilderness by a pillar of cloud in the day and by a pillar of fire in the night?
(Exodus 13:21)

_____

E

SSSSSSSSSSSSSSSSSSSSSSSSSSSSSSS

Each phrase below suggests a biblical person, place, or thing that begins with the letter S. Write each word by the proper number on the Ssssssssserpent . . . . . .

SSSSSSSSSSSSSS

1. The Devil
2. Later called Paul
3. A wise king
4. Hannah was his mom

SSSSSSSSSSSSSS

SSSSSSSSSSSSSS

5. Twin city to Gomorrah
6. A very strong man
7. Stoned as a martyr
8. Led the wise men to Jesus

SSSSSSSSSSSSSS **WORDS**

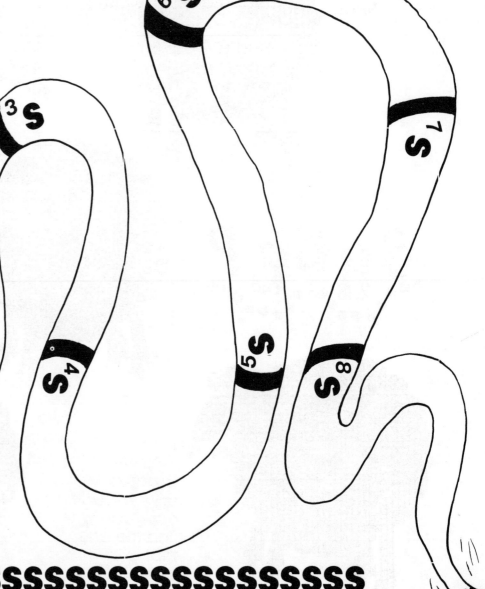

130

BAA BAA BLACK SHEEP

All the sheep are alike except one. Can you find the one that is different?

131

MOTHER'S DAY

Each mother has a baby sleeping in her arms. Use the list of children to name each mother's child.

Isaac
Jacob
John The Baptist

Jesus
Cain
Joseph

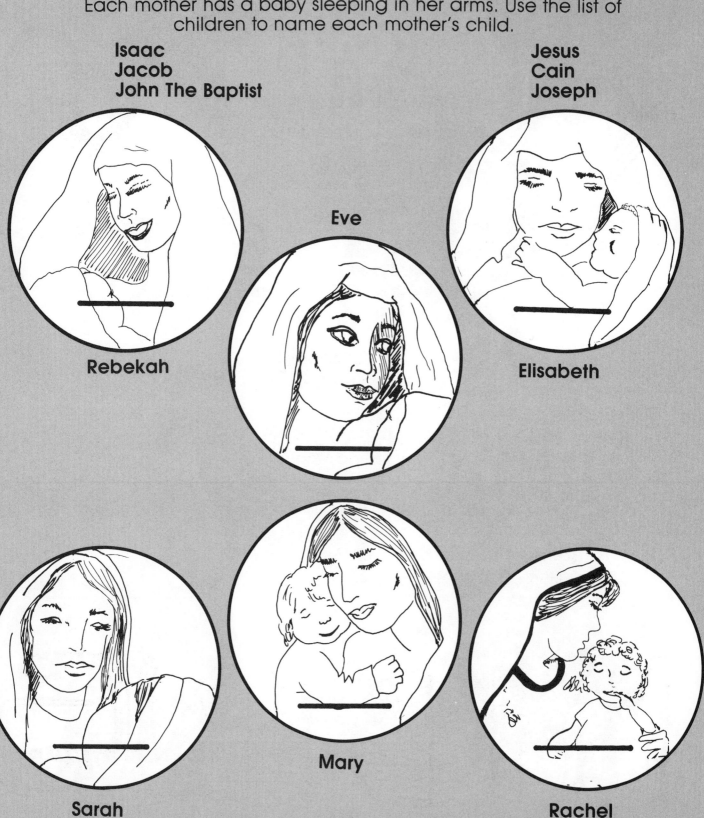

Eve

Rebekah

Elisabeth

Sarah

Mary

Rachel

132

Many animals are mentioned in the Bible. Ten of them are "hiding" in these nine sentences. Underline the ten animals' names.

Ex: You may prepare the cheese dish, or set the table.

1. Isn't that star amazingly beautiful?
2. The door might slam because the wind is strong.
3. My afro gets flat when I sleep on it.
4. I need the oleo; pardon me for reaching.
5. May I please borrow your masking tape?
6. We must be ready to go at three o'clock.
7. The traffic cop ignored the crowd and waved the bus through the intersection.
8. Doesn't she epitomize loveliness?
9. Nothing will undo good deeds done for others.

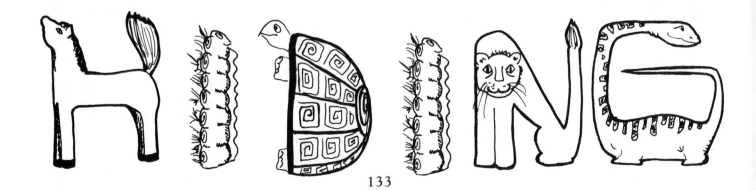

Read up, down, forward, backward, or diagonally to find these New Testament books:

```
B O O K S T R U S J X N
R E M S O I I T C O M A
S T A O F M C A R H O T
R E V E L A T I O N F H
A S U T I T H S S A G A
F I S U R T E M E L A N
I R O B H H K R A M L A
S E L U K E A O T T A R
H H A S K W B N E W T J
Y Y T R O A R T R R O I O
O S T U I J U D E T A Y
T E S T A M E N T W N C
H A H A H A I R O M A N S E
```

Acts   John   Jude
Galatians   Matthew   Hebrews
Revelation   Luke   James
Titus   Mark   Romans

SOMETHING FISHY

See if you can "catch" all the fish whose letters you see on the boat. Color them. Now look carefully at the letters you see on the plain fish, and you will be able to read a promise that Jesus made to Peter and Andrew.

Write the promise here:

___ ____ ____ ___ ___ ____ ____

___ ___ ____ ____ ___ ___ ___ . (Matthew 4:19)

135

E

Use this code to color the stained-glass window.

B = Blue   R = Red   G = Green   Y = Yellow   P = Purple

Now that you have finished, what do you see in the center of the window? Ask a friend to explain what it means, or look it up in the answer pages.

136

The LORD'S Prayer

The words in this list are spelled backward. Write each word correctly, then use the words to fill in the prayer that Jesus taught His disciples.

nevaeh _____   modgnik _____

lliw _____   yrolg _____

daerb _____   rewop _____

eman _____   htrae _____

stbed _____   noitatpmet _____

live _____

Our Father

Which art in _____,
Hallowed be thy _____.
Thy _____ come.
Thy _____ be done in _____, as it is in heaven.
Give us this day our daily _____.
And forgive us our _____, as we forgive our debtors.
And lead us not into _____, but deliver us from _____:
For thine is the kingdom, and the _____, and the _____,
for ever.

Amen.
(Matthew 6:9-13)

Fill in each space with an item that fits the category directly above the space and begins with the letter directly to the left of the space.

	BIBLE PEOPLE	BIBLE PLACES	BIBLE ANIMALS	BIBLE EVENTS
A				
B				
C				
D				

CROSS IT OUT

Follow the directions given in each sentence below. Then use the remaining letters to discover a special message, especially for you!

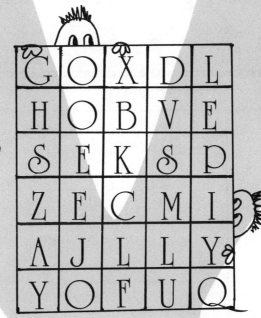

Cross out the letter that comes **first** in the name of the disaster that God brought to the people of Noah's world.

Cross out the letter that comes **first** in the name of God's son.

Cross out the letter that comes **first** in the name of Jesus' mother.

Cross out the letter that comes **first** in the official title of Esther in the Book of Esther.

Cross out the letter X.

Cross out the **first** letter in the name of the king who killed baby boys because he was jealous of Jesus.

Cross out the letter that comes **last** in the name of the 2nd book of the New Testament.

Cross out the **2nd** letter of the alphabet.

Cross out the **last** letter of the alphabet.

Write the message here: _____

FROM START to FINISH

Read these **"beginnings"** and **"endings"** and decide what event is being described. Choose your answers from the list given here. Write the number of your answer in the answer column. Use each event one time.

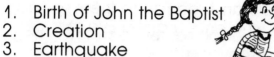

1. Birth of John the Baptist
2. Creation
3. Earthquake
4. Jesus' first miracle
5. Last Supper
6. Lord's Prayer
7. Red Sea crossing
8. Sermon on the Mount
9. Ten Commandments
10. Ten Plagues

Beginnings:	Endings:	Answers:
Our Father. (Matthew 6:9)	The glory, for ever. Amen.	
Beatitudes. (Matthew 5:3)	A parable (house built on a rock).	
A chariot chase. (Exodus 14:6)	An army drowned.	
There was light. (Genesis 1:3)	A day of rest.	
Marriage in Cana. (John 2:1)	Water turned to wine.	
A Passover feast. (Matthew 26:17)	A betrayer was revealed.	
Water turned to blood. (Exodus 7:20)	Death of the first-born.	
Paul and Silas in prison. (Acts 16:23)	The jailer's family was baptized.	
A priest became speechless. (Luke 1:20)	A prophet was born.	
Thou shalt have no other gods ... (Exodus 20:3)	Thou shalt not covet ...	

SsssLY GUY

Fill in the missing letter in the name of each Bible animal pictured. Then take those letters and rearrange them to find the name of the evil creature who encouraged Eve to disobey God.

lio _____   _____ agle   bi _____ d

grasshop _____ er

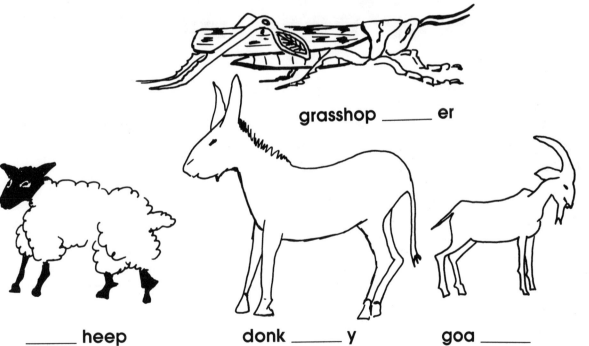

_____ heep   donk _____ y   goa _____

Now, who led Eve astray?

___ ___ ___ ___ ___ ___

SHADOW SHAPES

Elijah was an Old Testament prophet. A prophet was a person able to speak for God. One time God told him to go to a certain village where a widow would give him food. He did as God said, and he found the widow gathering sticks for a fire. He asked her for a cup of water and a piece of bread. She told him that she had no bread. She said she had only a handful of flour left in the sack and a little cooking oil in the bottom of a jar. The widow told Elijah she was gathering the sticks to build a fire for their last meal, and then she and her son would have to starve. Elijah said that if she would bake some bread for him, there would be plenty of oil and flour left for her and her son. She did as he said, and guess what! He was right. No matter how much she used, there was always plenty left, just as God had promised. The widow was very sure that Elijah was a man of God.

Later, the widow's son became very sick and died. Elijah asked God to help him bring the child back to life. The Lord heard Elijah, and the boy's soul returned to him. When the widow saw her son alive and well, she praised God.

Look at the shadow shapes in this picture. Name the things you see that are mentioned in the story of Elijah and the widow.

Can you find these things in the big picture? Draw a line from each one to its matching shadow shape.

AGENTS DOUBLE-O

You will need your Bible to do this activity.

Read all the sentences on this page before you begin to write!

Fill in the blank spaces at the end of the page. Then see if you can identify the key person or persons associated with each story. Write the name(s) in the space to the left of each sentence.

_____ 1. In Genesis 28:10-12, we went up and down a ladder.

_____ 2. In Matthew 28:2, we pushed a huge stone and then sat on it.

_____ 3. In Luke 1:11-13 and Luke 1:31, we made some very important announcements.

_____ 4. In Acts 12:21-23, we killed a proud New Testament king.

_____ 5. In II Samuel 24:10-16, we killed 70,000 people.

_____ 6. In Numbers 22:21-35, we used a donkey to get a man's attention.

(ODD & OUTLANDISH)

_____ 7. In Revelation 10:1-2, I am holding a little book.

_____ 8. In Genesis 19:1, 15-17, we rescued a man from a city that was being destroyed.

_____ 9. In Daniel 6:21-22, we shut some big mouths.

_____ 10. In Exodus 3:2, we were seen in a burning bush.

Write in these spaces the first letters of the Bible references in number 1, 3, 4, 6, and 10.

___ ___ ___ ___ ___
1   3   4   6   10

Now unscramble the letters to find out the name of the mysterious agents. _____

These agents have another very special job which they do every day — even now, in our time. Read Psalm 91:11 and Hebrews 1:14 to find out what this job is. Write your answer here.

Their special job is _____.

(ODD & OUTLANDISH)

145

THE A-B-SEEK GAME

A ___ ___

B ___ ___ ___

C ___ ___ ___ ___

D ___ ___ ___ ___ ___

E ___ ___ ___ ___ ___ ___ ___

F ___ ___ ___ ___

G ___ ___ ___ ___

H ___ ___ ___ ___

I ___ ___ ___ ___ ___ ___

J ___ ___ ___ ___ ___

K ___ ___ ___ ___

L ___ ___ ___ ___

M ___ ___ ___ ___ ___ ___ ___

N ___ ___ ___ ___ ___ ___

O ___ ___ ___

P ___ ___ ___ ___ ___ ___

Q ___ ___ ___ ___ ___

R ___ ___ ___ ___ ___ ___

S ___ ___ ___ ___

T ___ ___ ___ ___

Find on the opposite page a picture for each letter of the alphabet. Write its name in the correct space.

U ___ ___ ___ ___ ___ ___ ___

V ___ ___ ___ ___ ___

W ___ ___ ___ ___

___ X ___ ___

Y ___ ___ ___ ___

Z ___ ___ ___ ___ ___

When you have finished the game, choose two or three pictures about which you can tell a Bible story. Share them with a friend.

WORDS

An **epistle** is not

A feminine thistle,

Nor is an **apostle**

A biblical fossil.

The past tense of **Pharisee**

Is not pharisaw

But the **Pentateuch**

Is the five Books of Law.

Worship and **patriarch**

Are not kinds of boats,

And **Gospels**

Are not deeds by witches.

A **deacon** is not

A light on a steeple,

And a **church,** not a building,

But a group of God's people.

There are lots of unusual words in the Bible. Some are words we hear only in church. They are not part of our everyday conversation. That is why they seem so unfamiliar and difficult. Actually, most of them are not very hard to understand. Study this list of Bible words and their definitions. Then try the timed test on the next page to see how many you can remember, and return to this page to mark your score.

SCOREBOARD

Total time _____

Number missed_____

If you finished in twenty minutes or less and you missed fewer than ten matches, you are **A-OK!!**

If it took you longer than twenty minutes and you missed more than fifteen matches, study the list again. Then do the game again, trying to improve your score.

If you finished in fifteen minutes or less and you missed fewer than five matches, you are **SUPERSHARP!!**

Advent — the arrival of something awaited with anticipation, such as the birth of Christ.

apostles — disciples who are special messengers.

Beatitudes — short declarations that begin with "happy" or "blessed." (Part of the Sermon on the Mount.)

Bible — the Books, the Scriptures.

blessed — happy.

born-again — believing in Christ, thus becoming a member of God's family.

Christian — a person who believes in Jesus Christ as his Savior and Lord.

church — a group of God's people.

covenant — an agreement between two or more people.

deacon — someone who serves.

disciple — a learner or follower.

Epistles — letters that became twenty-one different Books of the New Testament.

exodus — a going out (as the Israelites' Exodus from Egypt).

faith — belief or trust that does not depend on material evidence.

gospel — Good News or the story about God.

the Gospels — the first four Books of the New Testament.

hallowed — honored.

magnify — praise.

manifested — shown.

Messiah — promised Savior.

miracles — wonders, signs, powers, and works of God.

Passover — a religious holiday for the Jews.

patriarch — father (such as Abraham, Isaac, and Jacob).

Pentateuch — the first five Books of the Bible.

Pharisees — members of a group of Jewish priests who were very strict about the religious laws.

priests — men who took the people's requests to God and God's will to the people.

prophet — an authoritative teacher of God's will.

rabbi — a teacher of Jewish law.

repent — to be sorry for sin and to turn away from it to God.

resurrection — a rising from the dead, returning to life.

the Revelation — an "unveiling" of the great events to come in the future.

Sadducees — a group of Jewish priests who did not believe in life after death.

Sanhedrin — the Jewish supreme court.

sepulcher — tomb

synagogue — a building where Jews meet to worship and study.

testament — a promise or covenant.

Trinity — the three persons of God: God, the Father, God the Son, and God the Holy Spirit.

worship — giving reverent love, devotion, and praise to God.

For Thinkers Only ...

Match each word in Column I with its proper definition in Column II by writing the correct number on each line. Ask someone to time you.

COLUMN I

1. covenant
2. Trinity
3. church
4. hallowed
5. worship
6. deacon
7. Pentateuch
8. miracles
9. gospel
10. resurrection
11. Epistles
12. Bible
13. born-again
14. prophet
15. exodus
16. patriarch
17. the Gospels
18. Beatitudes
19. Advent
20. blessed
21. Pharisees
22. Sadducees
23. disciples
24. faith
25. apostles
26. priests
27. sepulcher
28. Sanhedrin
29. rabbi
30. Christian
31. repent
32. magnify
33. manifested
34. Messiah
35. Passover
36. synagogue
37. testament
38. the Revelation

COLUMN II

____the arrival of something awaited with anticipation

____disciples who are special messengers

____the Books, the Scriptures

____short declarations that begin with "happy" or "blessed"

____the first four books of the New Testament

____believing in Christ, thus becoming a member of God's family

____a person who believes in Jesus Christ as his Savior and Lord

____a group of God's people

____an agreement between two or more people

____someone who serves

____a learner or follower

____letters that became twenty-one books of the New Testament

____a going out

____belief or trust that does not depend on material evidence

____Good News or the story about God

____honored

____praise

____shown

____promised Savior

____wonders, signs, powers, and works of God

____a religious holiday for the Jews

____father

____the first five books of the Bible

____a group of Jewish priests, strict about laws

____an authoritative teacher of God's will

____men who took people's requests to God and God's will to people

____a teacher of Jewish law

____to be sorry for sin and to turn away from it to God

____a rising from the dead, returning to life

____an "unveiling" of great future events

____Jewish priests who did not believe in life after death

____the Jewish supreme court

____tomb

____a building where Jews meet to worship and study

____a promise or covenant

____the three Persons of God

____giving reverent love, devotion, and praise to God

____happy

Women's Lib, B.C. ...

Before Israel had kings, it was once ruled by a woman. The people came to her for judgment as she sat under a palm tree. She was considered a very wise person, and led her people to a great victory over the Canaanites, who made life miserable for the people of Israel.

Look at the pictures on the left. Then write the name of each picture in the spaces opposite it. When you finish, you will find the name of this famous woman judge in the shaded spaces.

You can read the story of this lady judge in Judges 4 in your Bible.

Look carefully at each of the rebus pictures below and try to discover a Bible word. Write the word in the space beside the picture.

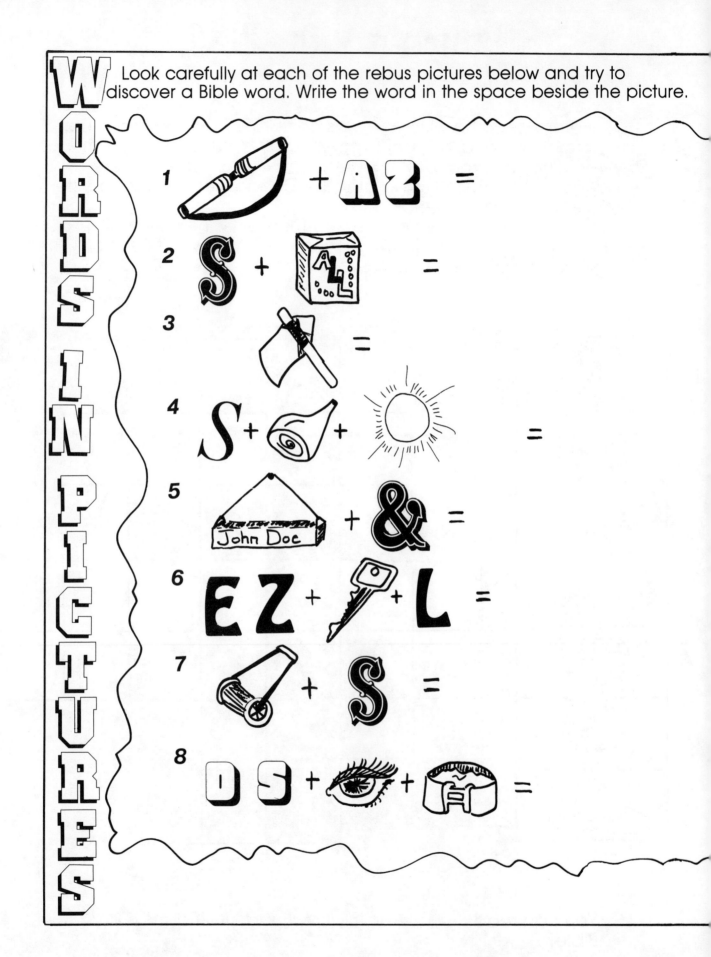

1   + A Z =

2   S +   =

3   =

4   S + +   =

5   John Doe + & =

6   E Z + + L =

7   + S =

8   O S + +   =

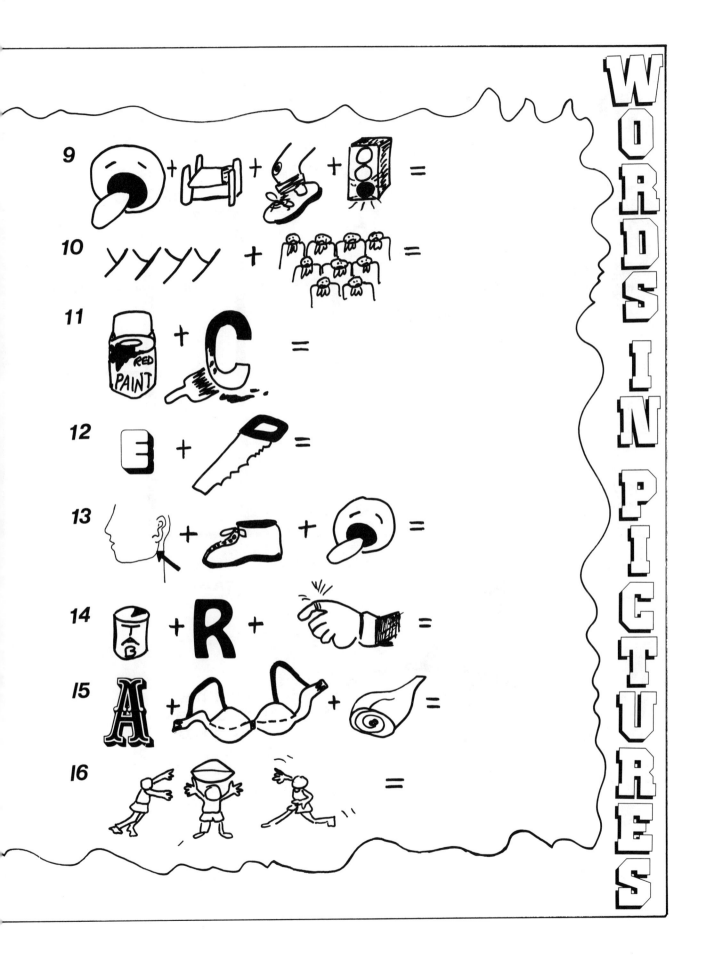

SINGLE LINE SYMBOLS

Can you draw each of these symbols without taking your pencil off the paper, without crossing any lines and without tracing over any lines?

The **cross** is a Christian symbol which reminds us Christ died for us.

The **fish** was used by the early Christians as a secret symbol to help them identify each other. They had many enemies who made it dangerous to be a Christian.

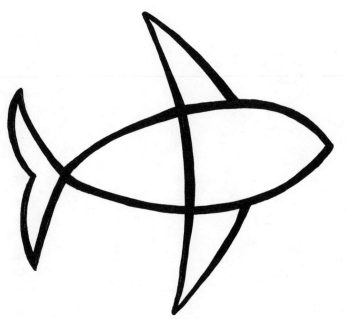

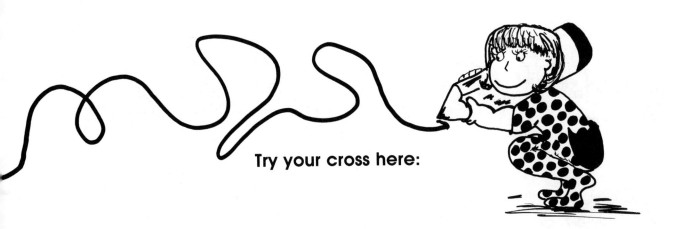

Try your cross here:

Try your fish here:

Look at these only if you need help:

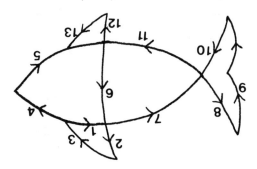

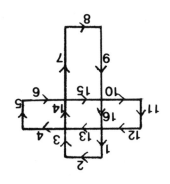

DELECTABLE

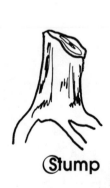

Cactus

Lake

One day, two Hebrew children asked their mother to help them think of a game to play. She made them a special map to follow for a treasure hunt. Read the directions and use a pencil to trace their path on the map to see where they found the treasure. Then write all the circled letters in the space below and unscramble them to find out what the treasure was!

Answer: ___ ___ ___ ___   ___ ___ ___ ___ ___

Stump

Grandmother's House

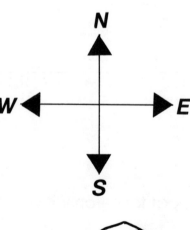

N

W ◄────┼────► E

S

Rock

TREASURE!

Berry Patch

Well

Cave

Begin at something prickly.
Hike southeast to a high peak where, often, there is snow.
Now go northwest and take a swim in a cool pool.
Search the inside of a hollow tree to the southwest.
Perhaps the treasure is hidden under plump, red berries in
    the north!
Or it's squashed flat under a heavy stone to the southwest.
Have you looked in a dark, scary, eastern place?
Scramble south to a row of posts.
Now go north to a deep, watery hole.
If you haven't found the treasure yet, try a trip southwest to
    the home of a very special friend.

Be sure to write the circled letter from the name of each
place you have visited on the lines; then unscramble the
letters to find the treasure!

Mountains

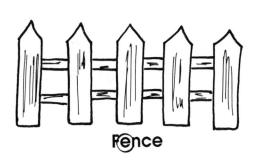

Fence

MAMMAL SCRAMBLE

1 Simon Peter should have stuffed
His big mouth with a sock.
He denied his Lord three times
Before the crowing of a

_____ .
KOCC

2 Daniel was found praying
By eyes that were a spyin',
Then tattling tongues informed the king
Who threw him to the

_____ .
NILO

3 From the deck of the ark,
Noah looked above
Then, off to find land,
He sent a _____ .
VODE

4 Jonah wouldn't have gone to Nineveh
If he had had his wish,
But God taught him obedience
In the belly of a _____ .
HSIF

5 A fire is usually set
With sticks or old papers and boxes,
But Samson set fire to the Philistines' fields
By lighting the tails of _____.
SOXFE

6 With David as their shepherd,
His sheep had the finest care.
Once he rescued them from danger
By killing a hairy, old _____ .
REAB

Complete each poem by unscrambling the name of the animal in bold print.

158

MAMMAL SCRAMBLE

7 Isaac was to be sacrificed
By his father Abraham
But, to take his place,
   in a bush nearby,
God placed a little _____.
MAR

8 Elijah sat wearily at the brook.
   Food and rest he was a cravin',
So God took care of his
   prophet's need
And fed him by means of a

_____ .
NEVAR

9 The Prodigal Son told his
   father,
"I want right now what is
   mine!"
But he quickly wasted it all
   away,
And ended up feeding

_____ .
SEWIN

10 Seek sound advice,
   For goodness' sake
Don't copy Eve
And obey a _____.
KESAN

11 Elijah proved to the prophets of Baal
That their God was a fake and a fraud.
He built an altar, then watered it down,
And prayed to the one true God.
The water covered the sticks and the stones.
The ditch 'round the altar was full.
But the fire came down and ate it ALL,
Including the sacrificed _____ .
LULB

12 When God says something will be, IT WILL BE!
He plagued Egypt with lizards and frogs.
And He kept His word about Jezebel's death,
For her body was eaten by _____ .
SODG

159

This game is a fun way to play TICK-TACK-TOE all by yourself. Fill each square on the TICK-TACK-TOE board with an **X** or **O** by choosing from each pair of Bible events the one which **happened first.** Place the proper letter **X** or **O** in the square which has the same number as that pair of events.

The object of the game is to see who wins — the **X**'s or the **O**'s and on which pair of events the game ends.

If you would like to have a friend play too, ask him or her to copy the board and number the squares like this one. Your friend may use the same list of events. See who picks the correct winner in the least amount of time!

WHICH HAPPENED FIRST????

X   O

1.	Samson loses his hair	**OR**	John the Baptist loses his head.
2.	Moses survives the crossing of the Red Sea	**OR**	Noah survives the great flood.
3.	Joseph marries Mary	**OR**	Abraham marries Sarah.
4.	Naaman washes away his leprosy in the Jordan River	**OR**	John the Baptist baptizes Jesus in the Jordan River.
5.	God gives the law to Moses (Ten Commandments)	**OR**	Christ gives the model for prayer (The Lord's Prayer).
6.	Lazarus is raised from the dead	**OR**	Christ rises from the grave.
7.	Christ disappears into heaven on a cloud	**OR**	Elijah disappears in a chariot of fire.
8.	Peter dreams of a great sheet filled with animals being lowered from heaven	**OR**	Jacob dreams of angels going up and down a ladder.
9.	Three Hebrew boys are thrown into a furnace because they obey God	**OR**	Stephen is stoned because of his faith in God.

THE FRAME GAME

Color the frames around the pictures that show activities which make Jesus happy.

THREE WICE, HAT'S NICE

Fill in the spaces with words that fit the definitions. Each of the three words will appear twice and will read the same from top to bottom and from left to right.

1. The animal mentioned in Matthew 19:24 _____
2. We must account to God for the things we have done, both good and _____
3. The animal's home mentioned in Daniel 6:7 _____

Great Tidings They Bring

There are some very special messengers from heaven.
Through them, many people in the Bible received important
news from God. You can read some stories about these
helpers in Matthew 1:20-21, Luke 1:11-20, and Luke 1:26-38.
Connect the dots to find out what these messengers might
have looked like.

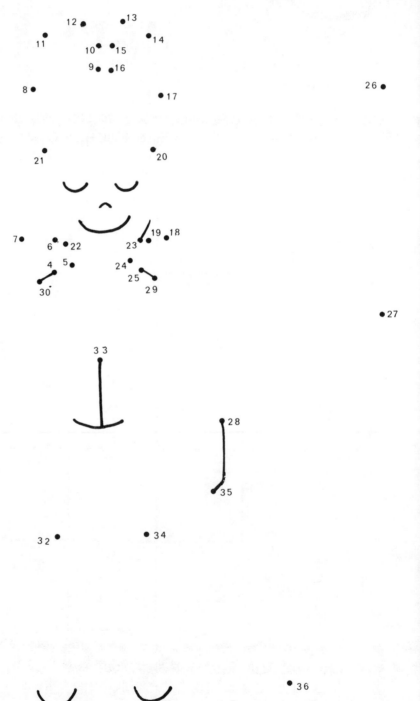

-CRET WORD-FIND

In this puzzle, there are 20 hidden Bible words which begin with a "C." They are spelled horizontally, vertically, diagonally, backward, and even diagonally backward. Can you circle all 20? They are listed below if you need help. After you have found them all, be sure you know their meanings. Try to remember where you have read these words in the Bible.

```
Y K C H A R I O T A Z C R K B T H
B M E R C H A P E L H E H O N L J
G N H C R U H C F D L B Z E C U M
J O G B W P Q M G Y I P M I R H W
A Q I C O V E N A N T D Z E U U I
R C A R O L B G C Y N L V N C C B
X C H R I S T U J A U H K O I H Q
M R L C K L V C M F M Q R E F R P
Q E V D O P A M V D S E G B Y I K
P A N U J R O X F W T F L X N S Q
V T K R A C R O W N C H A R I T Y
H I C V Q T U T E R N H K Y S M U
W O A R D V L P A D G K O P X A M
M N X G H C R O S S Q I B I B S H
B B W G C A N D L E K L N D R E V
J A R D C Z R T V C L E R G Y N J
```

camel, candle, caravan, carol, carpenter, chapel, chariot, charity, cherub, choir, Christ, Christmas, church, clergy, commandment, covenant, creation, cross, crown, crucify.

THE LINE-UP ...

See if you can identify each "criminal" by reading the description of his/her crime. Write the correct name on each one's I.D. tag.

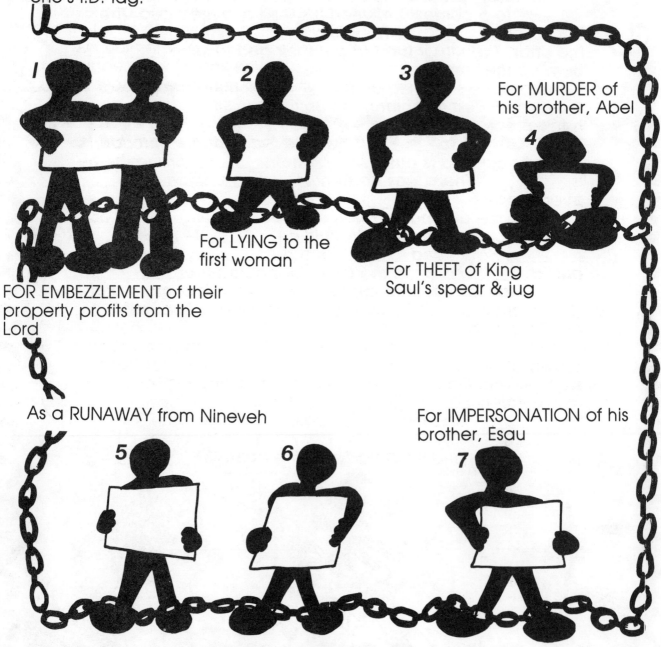

1 FOR EMBEZZLEMENT of their property profits from the Lord

2 For LYING to the first woman

3 For THEFT of King Saul's spear & jug

For MURDER of his brother, Abel

4 As a RUNAWAY from Nineveh

5 For acting as the ringleader in the KIDNAPPING of his brother, Joseph

6

7 For IMPERSONATION of his brother, Esau

ELIJAH LAUGHED AND LAUGHED

Complete this exciting story by reading 1 Kings 18:18-39 to find the missing words. Write a word in each space. Then read the story aloud to a friend. Use a strong voice, animated motion, and exaggerated expression!

One lonely prophet had challenged the 450 prophets of _____ to a contest between his God and their god. They built a great _____ . They laid _____ and a _____ on the altar. Then they tried to get their god to send _____ to burn up the sacrifice.

The prophets prayed and _____ . Nothing happened! They continued from morning until noon. Still _____ happened!

Elijah began to _____ . He hollered, "Louder ... louder! Maybe your god is busy. Maybe he is _____ or maybe he is _____ ." There was no sign of _____ . Elijah _____ even harder!

Late in the afternoon, Elijah stopped laughing. He called for everyone's attention. He built an _____ of twelve _____ . He placed _____ and a _____ on the altar. He dug a _____ around the altar. He poured four _____ of _____ on the meat to make it wet ... then four more and still another four, to be sure that it was nearly impossible for anything to burn.

Then, quietly, Elijah asked his _____ to show the great crowd of people and all the prophets of Baal whose God was the real God. SHAZAM!! Fire fell from heaven, and immediately ate up the _____ , the _____ , the _____ , the _____ , and the _____ that was in the ditch.

... and GOD had won the contest!!

167

Read 'N Write —

OH BAY

Y

THE

LORD 4 THIS IS R eye t.

E 6:1

Write the verse here in words.

_____

_____

_____

Read this verse, using the picture and letter symbols, then write it. Repeat it to yourself five times. Then try to say it without looking. If you have said it perfectly, give yourself a star here. ☐

A FAVORITE SON

I.

These pictures tell the story of Joseph, Jacob's favorite son,
but they are out of order. Number them in the right order.
Find a friend to whom you can tell this story.

For Thinkers Only ...

A Welcome Guest

Before Jesus left this earth to return to heaven, He promised His followers that He would not leave them alone, but would send a them a helper. The helper is the Holy Spirit.

The Holy Spirit is God's Spirit — just as Jesus is God's Son. He is part of God. He is one third of the Trinity. When a person becomes a Christian, the Holy Spirit comes to live within him. Sometimes He is called the Holy Ghost — perhaps because He cannot be seen — but He is not a scary creature. He is a very welcome guest.

To find out how the Holy Spirit helps Christians, see if you can interpret this mirror language. (You may try reading backwards or hold the page up to a mirror to read it.) Write each sentence correctly in the space provided.

The Holy Spirit helps Christians understand God's Word.
He gives them a special consciousness of what is right.
He helps them live as Jesus taught that His children should live.
He brings them courage and comfort when they are sad or afraid or troubled.

HOW THE HOLY SPIRIT HELPS CHRISTIANS:

1. _____

2. _____

3. _____

4. _____

TERSE VERSE

Can you think of a pair of rhyming words that go with each of the following definitions???

1. Jewelry belonging to a monarch. _____**King's rings**_____

2. Beds belonging to Abraham's nephew. _____

3. Flowers for the leader of Israel's people. _____

4. A shaved and bathed fisherman-disciple. _____

5. Large, hugging serpents on the ark. _____

6. Arms of the first woman's dress. _____

7. Horse barns belonging to one of the world's first brothers._____

8. The world's first murderer has headaches. _____

9. Clothing belonging to a very patient man._____

10. Believable stories told by Naomi's daughter-in-law._____

11. A quiet, peaceful verse of praise. _____

12. An Italian's way of expressing his love for a prophet.

_____

13. A minor prophet who was just fine!_____

14. How-to-do-it books belonging to a Hebrew captive.

_____

15. The bottoms of a prophet's feet. _____

16. A herdsman-prophet turned celebrity._____

For Thinkers Only ...

Each book on this page represents a Bible adventure story. Read the words on the "spine" or "backbone" of each book. Let these words remind you of a specific Bible adventure story you already know. Make up a title for that story and write it on the cover of the book.

Miracles

Water Turns To Wine

A Glad Dad

Stories of Strong Men

A Surprise Story

BIBLE   ADVENTURE

A Sad Story

A Happy Story

A Scary Story

Of Kings & Queens

A Special Baby Boy

Story of a Wicked City

LIBRARY

NO, NO, NOAH!!

An artist was asked to draw a picture about the story of Noah's ark. But she did not read the story very carefully, for she made many mistakes. Circle all the mistakes you can find. Then tell someone why they are wrong.

For Thinkers Only ...

THE NAME

In order to learn how to play this game:

1.   Choose the name of a Bible personality, and write it on the top line of the sample rectangle. Keep your choice a secret by covering it so your opponent cannot see it. The object of the game is to be the first player to circle all the letters in your secret name.

2.   Ask your opponent to do the same thing.

3.   Begin by calling one letter in your secret name. It does not have to be the first letter. Circle the letter as you call it. If the letter also appears in your opponent's secret name, he may circle it too.

4.   Now it is your opponent's turn to call a letter which appears in his secret name. He circles it as he calls it. If the letter appears in your secret name, you may circle it too.

5.   Keep a list of the letters your opponent calls on the second line of your rectangle.

At the beginning of your turn, you may choose to guess your opponent's secret name by observing this list. If you guess correctly, your opponent must start over with a new secret name. If your guess is incorrect, you lose your turn.

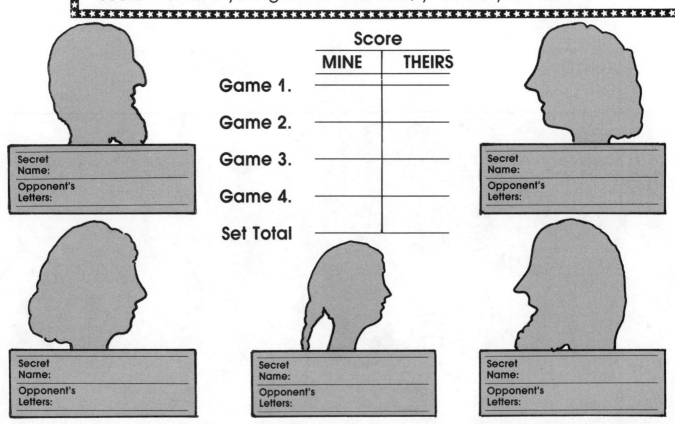

Score	MINE	THEIRS
Game 1.		
Game 2.		
Game 3.		
Game 4.		
Set Total		

Secret Name:
Opponent's Letters:

Secret Name:
Opponent's Letters:

Secret Name:
Opponent's Letters:

Secret Name:
Opponent's Letters:

Secret Name:
Opponent's Letters:

GAME!

(Your opponent gets the same opportunituy to guess your secret name when it is his turn.)

6. You may circle only one letter for each letter called. If a name has multiples of the same letter, that letter must be called more than once.

7. Continue taking turns calling letters until one of you has circled all the letters in your secret name. That person is then declared the winner.

Scoring:

The object of each single game is to be the first player to circle all the letters in your secret name. Your score for each game is the number of letters in your secret name — if you win. If you lose, you receive a score of 0 for that game. Total the scores of four games to find out who is the final winner of the set.

If you enjoy this game, make new rectangles on another piece of paper and play it as many times as you like.

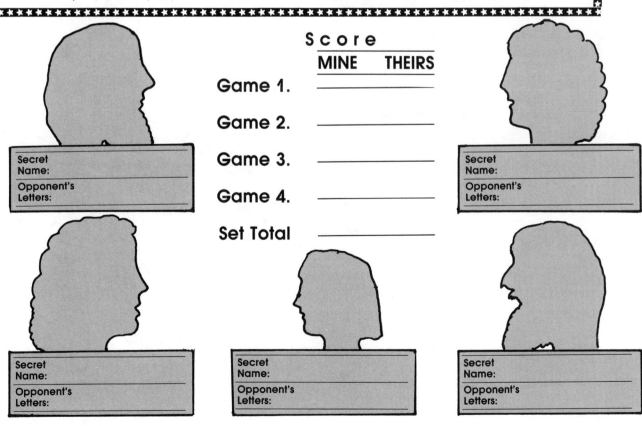

Score

	MINE	THEIRS
Game 1.		
Game 2.		
Game 3.		
Game 4.		
Set Total		

Secret Name:

Opponent's Letters:

Secret Name:

Opponent's Letters:

Secret Name:

Opponent's Letters:

Secret Name:

Opponent's Letters:

Secret Name:

Opponent's Letters:

BIBLE STORIES

The stories on this bookshelf are such exciting adventures that no boy or girl should miss reading them. Use this page as your checklist. As you complete each story, color the proper book. When you have read all the stories, you will have a lovely "library" of which to be proud.

A DONKEY TALKS! — Num. 22:1-38

Who is the real mother? — I Kings 3:16-28

A QUEEN SAVES HER PEOPLE — Esther

A Voice in the Night — I Sam. 3

Magic Oil & Flour — I Kings 17:8-16

A GOLD IMAGE AND A HOT FURNACE — Dan. 3

GREAT NEWS for the world — Luke 1:26-38, Luke 2:1-20

ESCAPE THROUGH THE SEA — EXODUS 14

CRAZY NOAH — Gen. 6:8-9:19

Elijah's Contest — I Kings 18

Escape from Jail — ACTS 12:1-17

NIGHT OF HORROR ... DAWN OF HAPPINESS — Matthew 26-28

AMAZE Your FRIENDS

One Shoe On and One Shoe Off
By ancient Hebrew law, if a man refused to marry his brother's widow, she was allowed to disgrace him by taking one of his shoes.
(Deuteronomy 25:9)

Better Than Wash 'n Wear!
During the 40 years that the children of Israel wandered in the desert, God saw to it that neither their clothes nor their shoes ever wore out.
(Deuteronomy 29:5)

A Year Off
By ancient Hebrew law, a man was not to be called to war or business during his first year of marriage. He was to be free to cheer up his wife.
(Deuteronomy 24:5)

Lucky Seven!
Some animals were taken on Noah's Ark in groups of seven. (Genesis 7:2)

Talk About Wrinkles!
Methuselah, the son of Enoch, lived to be 969 years old. (Genesis 5:27)

That's The Way To Go
There are two men in the Bible who never died. One was Enoch who was taken into heaven. (Genesis 5:21-22) The other was the prophet Elijah who was taken to heaven in a chariot of fire. (II Kings 2:11)

Amazing Animals
Balaam had a talking donkey. (Numbers 22:28) Jesus once got money to pay taxes from the mouth of a fish. (Matthew 17:27)

Maybe There Was One Without A Present
The Bible doesn't say there were three wise men. It only says that they brought three gifts. (Matthew 2:1,11)

God Must Have A Computer!
The hairs on each individual's head are numbered by God. If you pull one out, He changes His number. (Luke 12:7)

GOD In Ten Languages
French — Dieu
German — Gott
Spanish — Dios
Dutch — God
Japanese — Shin
English — Lord
Danish — Godh
Greek — Theos
Hindustani — Hakk
Mohammedan — Alla
(or Allah)

Crazy Pigs
A whole herd of pigs committed suicide by drowning themselves after demons entered them. (Matthew 8:31-32)

A Big Present
Solomon received an entire city as a wedding present from his new father-in-law, a Pharaoh. (I Kings 9:16)

The First King-Size Mattress
There was a king in the Bible who had a bed made of iron. It was over thirteen feet long and six feet wide. (Deuteronomy 3:11)

Far From Sweet
Lot's wife turned to salt when she disobeyed God. (Genesis 19:26)

Fish Story
Jonah was not necessarily swallowed by a whale — The Bible only says "a great fish." (Jonah 1:17)

Yuk!
People who worshiped idols ate mice. (Isaiah 66:17)

JUST PLAIN CORN

1. Where did Noah strike the very first nail in his ark?

2. When was tennis discussed in the Bible?

3. How many boiled eggs could Goliath eat on an empty stomach?

4. How did Jonah feel when the large fish swallowed him?

5. Which man in the Bible could have been the most successful doctor of all time?

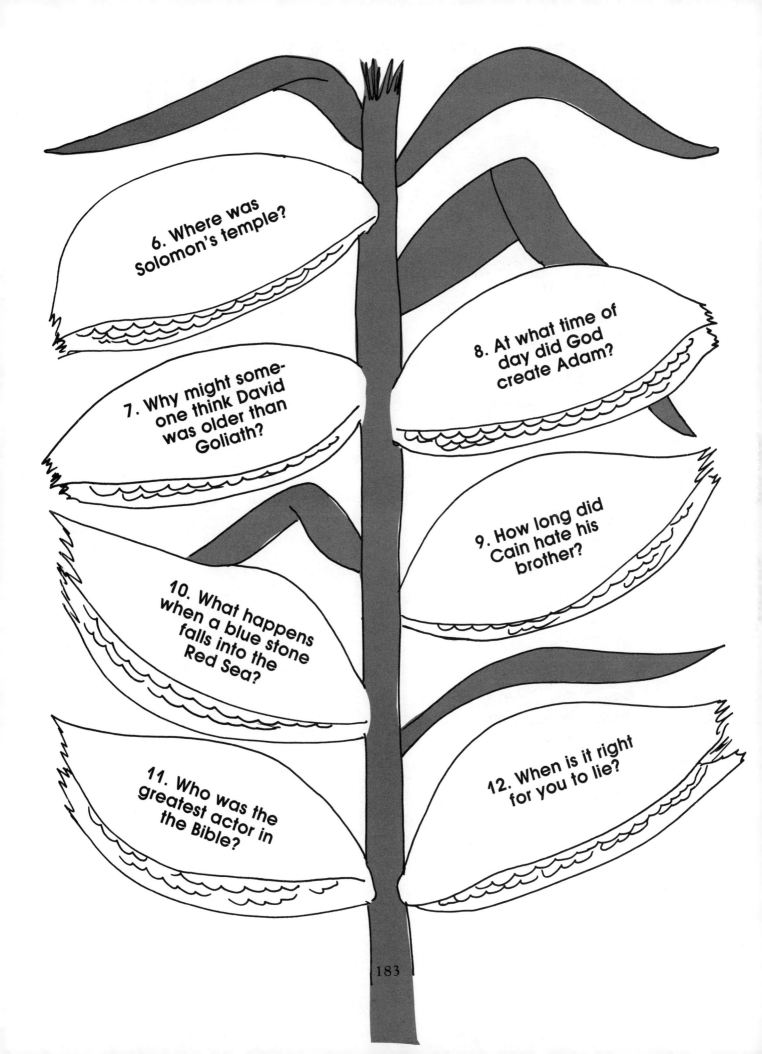

6. Where was Solomon's temple?

7. Why might some-one think David was older than Goliath?

8. At what time of day did God create Adam?

9. How long did Cain hate his brother?

10. What happens when a blue stone falls into the Red Sea?

11. Who was the greatest actor in the Bible?

12. When is it right for you to lie?

183

MORE CORN, Please!

Knock knock.
Who's there?
Atom.
Atom who?
Atom n' Eve.

Teacher: The President is married to the First Lady.
Boy: I thought Adam was!

What bow cannot be tied? (A rainbow)

What did God give to Adam that Adam could hold without touching it?

(His breath)

What is it that everyone has seen, but only God can ever see again?

(Yesterday)

What has eight legs, two hands, and wings?

(A man sitting on a donkey, carrying a bird.)

Peter: I caught 20 fish today, and I didn't even go fishing!
John: How could you possibly do that?
Peter: Andrew threw them to me.

When is a piece of wood like Queen Esther?

(When it is made into a ruler.)

John: What is the best way to keep old fish from smelling?
Andrew: Cut off their old noses.

What is in the very center of Jerusalem? (The letter s)

Dan and Stan studied about Noah's ark in Sunday School. On the way home, Dan asked, "Do you suppose old Noah did much fishing?" "How could he?" replied Stan. "He only had two worms!"

184

ANSWERS

Page 9 THE WORLD'S BIGGEST BELLYACHE

Page 11 THE CAREER CONNECTION

Joseph — carpenter
Luke — doctor
Jehu — chariot driver
Peter — fisherman
Nicodemus — rabbi
Caleb — spy
Solomon — king
Simon — magician
David — shepherd
Matthew and
Zacchaeus — tax collector
Jeremiah — prophet
Aquila — tentmaker
Gideon — soldier
Bartimaeus — beggar
Deborah — judge
Jezebel — queen
Abigail — a good wife
Haman — prime minister

Page 12 PICKIN' PEAS!!

Peter   Patmos   Philadelphia
Potiphar   Palestine   Prophets
Paul   Pilate   Pharaoh
Priscilla   Philip   Pharisees
Philistines

Page 13 WISE & WONDERFUL

Answers will vary.

Page 14 ANIMAL ACROSTIC

    B ee
    L i zard
    B ear
    L ocust
Hors e

    C a mel
  Do n key
    L i on
  La m b
  Sn a ke
  Wo l f
    S heep

Page 15 THE CASE OF THE LURKING LETTER

The "lurking letter" is **C.** The message is: A very important book is God's Holy Word, the Bible.

Page 16 CRACK THE CODE

Everyone who asks, receives; all who seek, find; and the door is opened to everyone who knocks.

Page 17 HOME SWEET HOME

No Answers

Page 18 TEST YOUR MEMORY

1. three
2. apple
3. leaves of a tree
4. two
5. two
6. a cat and a goat
7. a hill, camel, and four people
8. flowers
9. jug
10. two
11. sitting
12. shoes
13. two fish

Page 19 THE MICE ARE MISSING

Pages 20-21 A BALD HEAD IS BETTER THAN NO HEAD AT ALL

Page 20   Samson
            Jacob
Page 21   John the Baptist
            Paul

Pages 22-23 LEAPIN' LIZARDS

1. boils
2. death
3. locusts
4. hail
5. frogs
6. darkness
7. flies
8. lice
9. blood
10. diseased animals

Pages 24-25 CLOTHESLINE COUNTDOWN

Answers to these questions will depend on the extent of the reader's knowledge of these Bible characters. Therefore, there are no exact answers.

Pages 26-27 COMPARABLE PARABLES

Page 26   Good Samaritan
            Lost Sheep

Page 27   House Built on a Rock
            Other answers will vary

Pages 28-29 FAMOUS FAKES & TRICKS

1. Moses, bulrushes
2. Wife, bed, window
3. Solomon, mothers, child
4. Saul, wall, basket
5. Jacob, Esau, Issac
6. Salome, Herodias, John the Baptist, platter
7. Ananias, Sapphira
8. Delilah, hair
9. Laban, Leah, Rachel
10. David, insane

Pages 30-31 MIXED MATCH

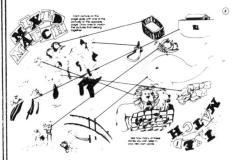

Pages 32-33 JUST THE RIGHT WORD

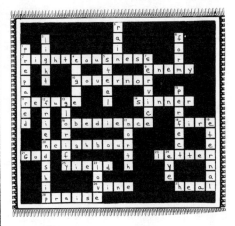

Page 34 TAG THE TOE

1. Peter
2. Moses
3. Paul
4. Zacchaeus
5. Goliath
6. Jesus

Page 35 FACTS IN FOURS

Answers will vary.

Page 36 THE PATHFINDER

Page 37 A STONE'S THROW

1. Saul
2. Thomas
3. Elijah
4. Peter
5. Hannah
6. Eli
7. Naaman

Page 38 FILM FANCY

The frames on this filmstrip tell the story of one of Jesus' miracles. However, the pictures are not shown in the order in which the events actually happened. Can you decide in what order the events occurred? Number the pictures, 1 through 5, in the small circle on each frame.

You can read this story in Matthew 9:2-8.

Page 39 A TREE FOR ZACH

Page 40 A TIMED TEST

John · Philip · Bartholomew
Peter · Thomas · James
James · Matthew · Simon
Andrew · Thaddeus · Judas

Page 41 REBUS RHYME

roses · lobe
frames · shark
fairy · ball
Spot · heater
tooth · rain

Page 42 GUESS WHO'S IN THE BUSHES

Ram

Page 43 PERPLEXED PROVERBS

"A soft answer turneth away wrath" (Proverbs 15:1)
"A wise son maketh a glad father" (Proverbs 15:20)
"A merry heart doeth good like a medicine" (Proverbs 17:22)

Page 44 NUTTY AS A FRUIT-CAKE

dates, grapes, honey, almonds, milk, flour, apples, walnuts, eggs, apricots, raisins, butter.

Page 45 W-WORD-WIDDLES

1. Work
2. Wait
3. Wisdom

Page 46 BIBLE SUPERLATIVES

1. Adam
2. Methuselah
3. 2 John
4. Samson
5. Goliath
6. Zacchaeus
7. Paul
8. Saul
9. Water turned to wine (wedding at Cana)
10. Cornelius
11. David
12. Genesis
13. Cain
14. Revelation
15. Manasseh
16. Solomon
17. Bible
18. Athaliah

Page 47 THE WAY TO HEAVEN

Except a man be born again, he cannot see the kingdom of God. John 3:3

Page 48 PUT-TOGETHER PARTS

2. Lazarus was Jesus' friend who rose from the dead.
3. Jehu commanded some men to throw a queen out a window.
4. Angels rescued from prison.
5. Nicodemus came to see Jesus at night.
6. A widow fed Elijah and increased her food supply.
7. Naaman dipped seven times in a river and was healed of leprosy.
8. Elijah had a contest with the prophets of Baal.
9. A wise king settled a fight between two mothers.
10. Joshua led a march around a wall.
11. Samuel was awakened in the night by a voice calling.
12. An earthquake destroyed a prison and a family found God.

Page 49 MIDNIGHT VISITOR

A very important man came to Jesus one night. He came at night because he didn't want his friends to see him. Jesus told him something strange. Jesus said, "You must be born again!" The man's name was Nicodemus.

To be born again means that you must be born as a child into God's family, just as you were born as a child into the family of your earthly parents.

Page 50 NO LIES-THAT'S WISE

1. F; Change *hospital* to *stable.*
2. F; Change *tigers* to *lions.*
3. T
4. T
5. F; Change *turtle* to *fish.*
6. T
7. F; Change *Daniel* to *Moses.*
8. F; Change *weak* to *strong.*
9. F; Change *girl* to *boy.*
10. F; Change *fire* to *flood.*
11. F; Change *pole* to *tree.*
12. T

Page 51 PUT CHRIST FIRST IN YOUR LIFE

C	H	R	I	S	T
h	o	e	d	c	r
u	m	c	e	h	a
r	e	e		o	v
c		s		o	e
h		s		l	l

Page 52 CHARACTER COMPOSITE

Answers will vary.

Page 53 NOW AND THEN

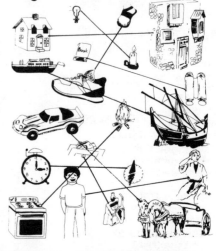

Page 54 PROPHET PUZZLER

Page 55 POEM PEOPLE

A male — Jonah
In a bed — a lame man
A goat — Noah
A mighty sling — David
A light — Saul
Something sweet — Mary of Bethany
The fall — Joshua
A "he" — Zacchaeus

Page 56 FACE UP

Answers will vary.

Page 57 RAIN-EE DAY

"When a man is gloomy, everything seems to go wrong; when he is cheerful, everything seems right!" (Proverbs 15:15 TLB)

Page 58 IT ALL STARTED WITH THE CREATION

ace	cent	inter	race	tare
acne	certain	ion	rain	tea
acorn	cite	iota	ran	tear
acre	coat	irate	rant	ten
act	con	ire	rat	tern
action	cone	iron	rate	tic
actor	core	it	ratio	tie
air	corn	near	ration	tier
an	cot	neat	react	tin
ant	crane	nice	reaction	tine
at	crate	nit	rent	tire
can	cretin	no	retina	to
cane	ear	nor	rice	toe
can't	earn	not	rite	ton
car	eat	note	roan	tone
care	eon	on	rot	tonic
cart	era	one	rote	tore
carton	ice	or	taco	torn
cat	icon	orate	tan	trace
cater	in	ore	tar	train
				trance

Page 59 WHAT A WORLD!
No answers.

Page 60 SORRY, WRONG NUMBER
1. Change 11 to 12.
2. Change 8 to 10.
3. Change 20 to 2.
4. Change 20 to 21.
5. Change 15 to 12.
6. Change 4 to 5.
7. Change 18 to 12.
8. Change 200 to 30.
9. Change 2 to 3.
10. Change 25 to 40.

Page 61 GIVE ME FIVE BOOKS
of the Bible: Answers will vary.

Riddles:
1. Jesus   3. Bible   5. Fruit
2. Angel   4. Faith

Bible Characters: Answers will vary.

Page 62 A SAFE TRIP HOME

The good Samaritan helped a man who was not his friend.
See if you can help this good man get all the way home
without meeting any robbers!

PAGE 63 TWIN BUTTERFLIES
The butterfly on the top right side of the page is exactly like the butterfly in the center.

Page 64 BEWARE! BEWARE!
Forgive my sins and cleanse from unrighteousness.

Page 65 SILHOUETTE SCRAMBLE
1. dragon   3. camel   5. lion
2. lamb   4. leopard

Page 66 ACTIONS DO TELL
Answers will vary.

Page 67 HE'S ALIVE!!
garden
angel
croses
thunder
Mary
soldiers
stone
Christ
Tomb
disciples
Joseph
forgiven

Page 68 THE SUN STOOD STILL; THEN IT MOVED BACKWARD!
No answers.

Page 69 JUMBLED JABBER
1. Wicked Delilah had Samson's hair cut while he slept. Omit **Baal.**
2. Daniel disobeys the king's command and is throw into a den of lions. Omit **window.**
3. Thou shalt love the Lord thy God with all thy heart. Omit **commandment.**
4. Nehemiah and his friends rebuilt Jerusalem's wall in 52 days. Omit **Babylon.**
5. Jarius' daughter was raised from the dead. Omit **servant.**
6. Gideon's army won the battle with horns and jars. Omit **Goliath.**
7. Do unto others as you would have them to unto you. Omit **golden.**
8. Balaam beat his donkey three times. Omit **angel.**

Page 70 CRISS-CROSS FUN
Answers: 1. Son; 2. One; 3. Net

Page 71 ME & MY DAD
1. F   4. A   7. D   10. I
2. C   5. H   8. E
3. J   6. B   9. G

Page 72 FISHERMEN FOUR
The fisherman on the far right caught the fish.

Page 73 A FAMILY TREE

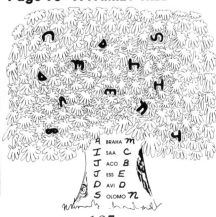

A BRAHA m
I SAA C
J ACO B
J ESS E
D AVI D
S OLOMO n

Page 74 HALF & HALF
1. Samson
2. Rachel
3. Martha
4. Esther
5. Dorcas
6. Andrew
7. Jairus
8. Ruth
9. Luke
10. Adam

Page 75 JIGSAW JUMBLE
LAMB OF GOD

Pages 76-77 COPY CAT
No Answers.

Page 78 NOAH'S SURPRISE

Page 79
"Noah has chosen us as the two rabbits to take on the ark. Ha! Ha!"

"What's so funny about that?"

"By the time we come out, there will be lots of us!"

Pages 80-81 A VERY OLD MESSAGE TOLD MANY NEW WAYS
No Answers.

Pages 82-83 LOTS O' LUGGAGE
Answers will vary.

Pages 84-85 FINDERS, KEEPERS

Page 84
1. crown
2. angel
3. bread
4. ape
5. candle
6. heart
7. rainbow
8. foot
9. needle
10. dove

Page 85
1. fish
2. bread
3. merry heart
4. dragon
5. coat
6. tree
7. cup
8. hand
9. cross
10. star

Pages 86-87 A PATH TO A BATH
NAAMAN	SEVEN	HEALTHY
LEPROSY	HEALED	GIFTS
GIRL	REFUSED	REAL
SAMARIA	OBEY	
ELISHA	SKIN	

Pages 88-89 WHAT'S IN A NAME?

Page 88
Adam
Abraham
Jacob
Bathsheba
Herod
Martha
Samson
James
Mark

Page 89
Naaman
Timothy
Philemon
Matthew
Abednego
Stephen
Cornelius
Caleb
Delilah
Barnabas

Pages 90-91 STRAIGHT A'S

Agrippa   Absalom
Adam   Abba
Abednego   Ararat
Abigail   Abraham
Ahab   Ananias
Achan   Andrew
Aquila   Arimathea
Abel

Pages 92-93 REBUS RIDDLES

1. Bible; 2. Jacob; 3. Noah;
4. Pilate; 5. Esther; 6. Adam;
7. Isaac; 8. Herod; 9. Enoch;
10. Jehu; 11. Eli; 12. Philip;
13. Haman

Pages 94-95 THE MAD CHARIOT RACE

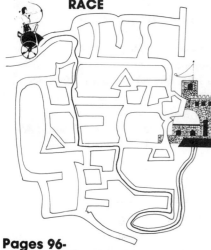

Pages 96-97 SOMETHING WONDERFUL

No Answers.

Pages 98-99 NAME THAT BOOK

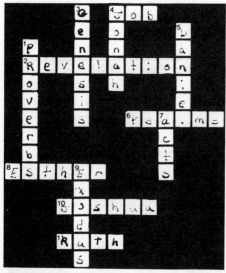

Page 100 DO YOU COMPUTE?

```
    3
 + 27
 - 12
 + 20
 - 10
 - 12
 - 12
 +  3
 -------
    7 Total
```

Page 101 REBUS ARITHMETIC

beehive + teeth - tie + camel - cave - 3 = Bethlehem

veil + dog + date - leg - toe = David

Page 102 THE FRAME-UP

Jesus did not sit on a throne and wear jewels.

Jesus did not get married.

Page 103 WHAT A NAME

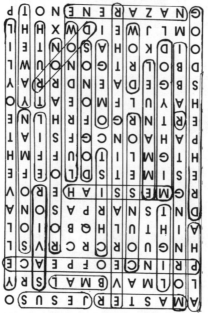

Page 104 GOD'S V.I.C.'S

The small creature is a sparrow.

Page 105 NO ROOM

Page 106 A SPECIAL SECRET

S A M S O N

Page 107 A MYSTERY MEAL

Page 108 CODED COMMANDMENTS

Love the Lord your God with all your heart, soul, and mind. The second is, love your neighbor as much as you love yourself. Keep only these and you will find that you are obeying all the others.

Page 109 THREE BY THREE

Answers will vary.

Page 110 SAY IT STRAIGHT

1. God loves you very much.
2. A light from heaven blinded Saul.
3. An angel helped Peter escape from jail.
4. A poor widow gave Elijah food.
5. Lazarus was raised from the dead.
6. Judas betrayed Jesus for 30 pieces of silver.

Page 111 GOOD NEWS

Jesus loves boys and girls. Yea!

Page 112 SOUND-ALIKES

One answer for each is given here; however, there are other acceptable answers.

Adam   Luke
Paul   Job
Peter   James
John   Hosea
Sarah   Samuel
Lot   Baal
Moses   Hannah
Stephen   Amos
Aaron   Cain
Noah   Jonah
Mary   Eve
Mark   Ham

Page 113 ODD MAN OUT

Cross Out:
1. *Job.* The others were in the New Testament.
2. *Paul.* The others were 4 of the original 12 disciples.
3. *Moses.* The others were sons of Jacob.
4. *Los Angeles.* The others were Bible cities.
5. *Peter.* The others were Old Testament prophets.
6. *Delilah.* The others were queens.
7. *Moriah.* The others were Bible mothers.
8. *Adam.* The others were kings.
9. *Snakes.* The others were Egyptian plagues.
10. *Ring.* The others were symbols of the Holy Spirit.
11. *Bottle of perfume.* The others were associated with miracles.
12. *Matthew.* The others were in the Old Testament.

Page 114 A KIND WORD PUZZLE

188

Page 115 HIDE & SEEK

1. Aaron
2. Amos
3. Cain and Abel
4. Lot
5. Matthew
6. Paul
7. Solomon
8. Mark
9. Luke
10. Thomas

Page 116 MASKED MESSAGE

We'll meet Friday to pray for Paul.

Page 117 IF YOU'RE HAPPY, SHOUT

H	A	L	L	E	L	U	J	A	H
1	2	3	4	5	6	7	8	9	10

Page 118 COLOR CAPER

Camel

Page 119 SOLOS, DUETS, & TRIOS

Solos:
David
Donkey
Daniel
Rahab
Mary

Duets:
Ruth, Naomi
Jacob, Esau
Moses, Aaron
Adam, Eve
Joshua, Caleb

Trios:
Shadrach, Abednego, Meshach
Father, Son, Holy Spirit

Page 120 STEPS TO SUCCESS

fear
　hear
　　head
　　　dead
　　　　read
　　　　　real
　　　　　　seal

"The **fear** of the Lord is the beginning of knowledge" (Proverbs 1:7).

Page 121 PICTURE PERFECT

Page 122 ONE ROYAL MESS!

1. JEZEBEL
2. ESTHER
3. BATHSHEBA
4. AHAB
5. SAUL
6. DAVID
7. SOLOMON

Page 123 FUNNY MONEY

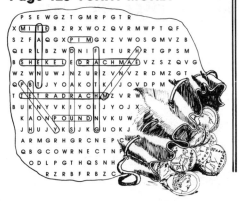

Page 124 A VERY SPECIAL STORY

Many people followed Jesus wherever He went. One day, five thousand people came to hear Him. It was meal time and they were hungry. Jesus took a boy's five loaves and two fish and made them stretch to feed all five thousand. There was plenty left over. How do you think He did it?

Page 125 ONLY ONE!

"There is one God, and one mediator between God and men, the man Christ Jesus" (I Timothy 2:5).

Page 126 PICTURE CROSSWORD

Page 127 EYES IN DISGUISE

Serpent

Page 128 WORDS TO THE WISE

sun　　down　　angry

"Don't let the sun go down with you still angry" (Ephesians 4:26 LB).

Page 129 ALL FIRED UP

1. Moses
2. Samson
3. Sodom and Gomorrah
4. Elijah
5. Jesus
6. Israelites

Page 130 SSSS WORDS

1. Satan
2. Saul
3. Solomon
4. Samuel
5. Sodom
6. Samson
7. Stephen
8. Star

Page 131 BAA, BAA, BLACK SHEEP

The sheep in the lower right-hand corner of the page is different.

Page 132 MOTHER'S DAY

Rebekah — Jacob
Eve — Cain
Elisabeth — John the Baptist
Sarah — Isaac
Mary — Jesus
Rachel — Joseph

Page 133 ANIMALS IN HIDING

1. ram
2. lamb
3. frog
4. leopard
5. ape
6. goat
7. pig, crow
8. sheep
9. dog

Page 134 BOOK LOOK

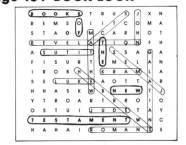

Page 135 SOMETHING FISHY

"I will make you fishers of men." (Matthew 4:19).

Page 136 COLOR TIME

In the center of the window, you should see a white dove. The dove is probably the most common symbol of the Holy Spirit.

Page 137 THE LORD'S PRAYER

Our Father
Which art in heaven,
Hallowed be *Thy name*
Thy Kingdom come.
Thy will be done in earth, as
it is in heaven.
Give us this day our daily bread.
And forgive us our debts, as we forgive
our debtors.
And lead us not into temptation, but
deliver us from evil:
For thine is the kingdom, and the power,
and the glory for ever.
　　　　Amen

Page 138 FOUR BY FOUR

Answers will vary.

Page 139 CROSS IT OUT!

God loves especially you!

Page 140 FROM START TO FINISH

Our Father — 6
Beatitudes — 8
A chariot chase — 7
There was light — 2
Marriage in Cana — 4
A Passover feast — 5
Water turned to blood — 10
Paul and Silas in prison — 3
A priest became speechless — 1
Thou shalt have no other gods — 9

Page 141 SSSSLY GUY

n, e, r, p, s, e, t = serpent

Pages 142-143 SHADOW SHAPES

Pages 144-145 AGENTS DOUBLE O

1. Jacob
2. Jesus
3. Zacharias, Mary
4. Herod
5. David
6. Balaam
7. John
8. Lot
9. Daniel
10. Moses

G	L	A	N	E
1	3	4	6	10

Angel

Their special job is to protect, guard, and minister to Christians.

Pages 146 -147 THE A-B-SEEK GAME

Ark	Jonah	Star
Bible	King	Tomb
Cross	Lion	Unicorn
Dragon	Menorah	Viper
Elephant	Numbers	Well
Frog	Old	aXe
Goat	Pyramid	Yoke
Horn	Queen	Zebra
Island	Rainbow	

Pages 148 -150 BIG, SCARY, RELIGIOUS WORDS

Pages 148 -149

No Answers

Page 150

19	8
25	35
12	16
18	7
17	21
13	14
30	26
3	29
1	31
6	10
23	38
11	22
15	28
24	27
9	36
4	37
32	2
33	5
34	20

Page 151 WOMENS LIB, B.C.

Door
Bell
Book
Clouds
Grapes
Pear
Hat

Pages 152 -153 WORDS IN PICTURES

1. Boaz; Saul; 3. Acts;
4. Samson; 5. Naaman;
6. Ezekiel; 7. Moses; 8. Disciple; 9. Abednego; 10. Wise men; 11. Red Sea;
12. Esau; 13. Joshua; 14. Tabernacle;
15. Abraham; 16. Passover.

Pages 154 -155 SINGLE-LINE SYMBOLS

No Answers.

Pages 156 -157 DELECTABLE TREASURE!

Honey cakes.

Pages 158 -159 MAMMAL SCRAMBLE

1. Cock	7. Ram
2. Lion	8. Raven
3. Dove	9. Swine
4. Fish	10. Snake
5. Foxes	11. Bull
6. Bear	12. Dogs

Pages 160 -161 X - O - X

7 O	1 X	6 X
4 X	3 O	2 O
5 X	9	8 O

O wins on number eight.

Page 162 THE FRAME GAME

1. Teasing animals does not make Jesus happy.
2. Mistreating other people does not make Jesus happy.

Page 163 THREE TWICE, THAT'S NICE

1. Camel
2. Bad
3. Den

Page 164 GREAT TIDINGS THEY BRING

These messengers are angels.

Page 165 C-CRET WORD-FIND

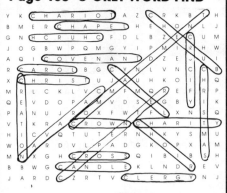

Page 166 THE LINE-UP

1. Ananias and Sapphira
2. Satan
3. David
4. Cain
5. Jonah
6. Reuben
7. Jacob

Page 167 ELIJAH LAUGHED AND LAUGHED

1. Baal	14. stones
2. altar	15. wood
3. wood	16. bull
4. bull	17. ditch
5. fire	18. jars
6. danced	19. water
7. nothing	20. God
8. laugh	21. bull
9. traveling	22. wood
10. sleeping	23. stones
11. fire	24. soil
12. laughed	25. water
13. altar	

Page 168 READ 'N WRITE

"Children, obey your parents in the Lord: for this is right" (Ephesians 6:1).

Page 169 A FAVORITE SON

6	5
1	3
4	2

Page 170 A WELCOME GUEST

Use a mirror to find the answer.

Page 171 TERSE VERSE

1. King's rings; 2. Lot's cots;
3. Moses' roses; 4. neater Peter; 5. Noah's boas; 6. Eve's sleeves; 7. Abel's stables;
8. Cain's pains; 9. Job's robes; 10. Ruth's truths; 11. calm psalm; 12. I lika' Micah!;
13. O.K. Hosea; 14. Daniel's manuals; 15. Joel's soles;
16. famous Amos.

Pages 172 -173 BIBLE ADVENTURE LIBRARY

Answers will vary.

Pages 174 -175 NO, NO, NOAH!!

Pages 176 -177 THE NAME GAME

No answers.

Pages 178 -179 BIBLE STORIES TOO GOOD TO MISS

No answers.

Pages 180 -181 AMAZE YOUR FRIENDS

No answers.

Pages 182 -183 JUST PLAIN CORN

1. On the head.
2. When Joseph served in Pharoahs court.
3. None, because after the first bite, his stomach wasn't empty.
4. Down in the mouth.
5. Job — he had more patience (patients) than any other man.
6. On the side of his head.
7. David, since he rocked Goliath to sleep.
8. Just before Eve.
9. Just as long as he was Abel.
10. It gets wet.
11. Samson — he brought the house down.
12. When you go to bed.

Page 184 MORE CORN, PLEASE

Answers on P. 184.

INDEX